Trevor Towill

The Loveable Rogue

ISBN: 978-1-911412-90-8
Apple: 978-1-911412-89-2
Kindle: 978-1-911412-92-2

BookPublishingWorld
An imprint of Dolman Scott Ltd
www.dolmanscott.co.uk

Trevor Towill –
The Loveable Rogue

21st April 1960 was the day that someone decided was a good time for me to be inflicted on my parents or indeed on the whole of the human race! This all happened at the Churchill Hospital in Oxford to my parents Michael William and Joan Ann. They were both over the moon that I was a boy following my sister Susan Ann. They proudly brought me home to Poplar Grove in Kennington, Oxford.

My earliest memories are of my 2nd Christmas when an auntie Pat arrived at our house with an enormous box and when I opened it I was amazed to see a beautiful blue and white lorry carrying milk churns. I remember playing with that lorry for many months.

The snow was on the ground that year- it was one of those terrible years when it never seemed to stop. My dad was driving our large grey van going between Kennington and Botley and my sister and I were in the passenger seat at the front. The drifts had reached 12 –15 feet along the road when a red mini came towards us sliding all over the road. It hit the driver's side of our van and after it had bounced off it, it completely buried itself in the snowdrift. The snow continued for many months.

My dad at the time was working at BMC motors in Cowley. He was building cars on the assembly lines with one of his elder brothers and his youngest sisters husband. In the July of 63 the factory closed down for summer holidays and we set off to Cornwall with the Godbold Family who were an aunt and uncle of mine and their two children. We arrived first ahead of the other family as my dad was driving his Jaguar car and they only had a maroon Riley 1.5

The sea stretched out ahead of us- I loved it and all I wanted to do was play in the sand and the sea. I certainly didn't like it when I was told it was time to go back to the caravan I remember crying and screeching at the top of my voice. What an amazing holiday we had.

I cannot remember the rest of that year but at Christmas we had a big family party with all the Uncles and Aunts and cousins and grandparents. These were good family memories that a lot of people do not have.

In 1964 I was allowed out on my own! I used to walk to the top of Poplar Grove, wait for the milkman who would let me come down in his milk float. Mum used to watch this all happening but I thought it was great. It went on for a long time and I was given the nick name Trevor Bot Bot. Around this time one thing I remember very vividly is the day when I climbed into the back of Dad's van, buried myself in blankets and went into a deep sleep and whilst this was happening my family and neighbours were looking for me. Then the police were called in to help. I was only 4 at the time and the railway line was quite close and the river also was nearby. My dad drove around the local streets looking for me for about

45 minutes I awoke suddenly and sat behind my dad whilst he was driving. He got me back home to screeching and crying that I had been found, although to this day I don't know why they were crying. I was a naughty little sod then when I think about it. I probably got a telling off for that little episode but would have soon got over it.

My dad had a smallholding up the road where there was a little lane called Cow Lane. He had pigs and goats and chickens and was growing lots of fruit and vegetables. I used to love it down there, I was always getting dirty-I was in my element. Back at home we had a big barn in our garden and lots of chickens and ducks running around. In that barn Dad put up a swing from the rafters and that soon attracted all the kids around the neighbourhood. I had lots of friends then, probably because of the swing!

On 20th March 1964 my younger sister Sarah Joan was born. During that summer we all trouped down to Cornwall again and had a wonderful 10 days. It was another amazing adventure for me as it meant going back to the seaside

Approaching 1965 and of course it was time for me to go to school. Every day my parents would take me in I would find a way out through another entrance and be sat on the doorstep of our home by the time my mother returned and subsequently she would march me back to school again.

In September 1965 my grandmother died. She lived opposite us in Poplar Grove. I remember her as being a very stern woman that stuck her nose into other people's business, especially my parents. When it came to the children she knew best particularly with me! I can remember her slapping me on several occasions when I said something out of turn.

Following this event my mum didn't want to stay in Oxford so dad suggested that perhaps we could move, maybe go near to the sea. A month or two went by and to my parents surprise there was an advert in the local paper regarding a family that wanted a council exchange from the Isle of Wight to Oxford. They both worked on the Island buses and at the time they had seen an advertisement for the Oxford City buses that paid more than the island did.

In the March of 1966 we headed over to the island to view the house at 61, Binstead Road, Ryde. It was the first time I had actually been on a boat coming over on the ferry from Portsmouth, what an adventure, I loved it. After viewing the house the Egbee's I think they were called, took us down to the beach at Binstead. We were all really excited and all that was left was for the Egbees to come and see our house in Oxford.

By the time they came back to see us they already secured jobs and once they saw the house that was it. We were moving over to the Isle of Wight!!

By June all the packing was done, the removal lorry was loaded and I sat with my sisters in my dad's car. The neighbours all came out waving and in tears, that was probably tears of joy as I was leaving the area. I really was a little bugger then. My mum was in Uncle Will's car with our little pet cat Fluffy and we headed to Portsmouth to catch the old car ferry to Fishbourne. I remember the ferry being called The Camber Queen and it was 1pm in the afternoon. About 45 minutes later we arrived and had 2 miles to cover before we reached our new home.

After disembarking from the ferry at Fishbourne we only had a five-minute drive to our new home at 61, Binstead Road, Ryde. When we arrived it was time for us all to help to put things into respective rooms in the house. Of course all I wanted to do was get down to the beach however I did help under sufferance and about 7pm I got my wish and we ended up at the beach. At Binstead there were lots of rock pools, I was fascinated as the tide was coming in, the sea was moving and I kept thinking when the tide goes out where does all the water go? From that early age, 6 at the time, I knew that my life would revolve around the sea. I was buzzing, asking lots of questions, which of course my parents really didn't know the answers-; none of us had lived by the sea before that day.

All the neighbours came round and introduced themselves, everyone seemed so friendly and welcoming but they didn't know me yet, they didn't realise what a devil I could be.

I remember that first week very clearly; going out in the car to have a look around and the beauty of it really struck me even at that age. Going under the pier at Ryde with the train over the top of us, the trams and people walking and even cars going up the pier to park to drop passengers off for the ferry to the mainland. It was fascinating to a youngster, all this amazing stuff going on around me.

The following week it was time for me to go to school –again I escaped and used to arrive back home before my parents reached our house. Time and time again they took me back and eventually I had to stay for the duration and just put up with it. Needless to say it was totally against what I wanted to do which was go to the beach.

A few days later we were down at the beach when we met a family who were picking up cockles for their supper, They got chatting to my parents and became great friends. Dave and Kay Long and their 4 children. During that time we all spent a lot of time together. Once we went down to Compton Bay on the south west coast of the island and remember huge waves coming in –it was fantastic, I loved it. It was here that we found a shark that had got swept onto the beach from the big waves. It was about 4 foot long and was still alive. My dad walked into the sea and released it back into it's environment. What a wonderful time we were all having, a whole new life ahead of us.

The Long family lived just around the corner from us. A couple of days a week we would collect cockles for our supper. Our dad was still commuting back to Oxford on Sunday night to return on the Friday afternoon. After a few weeks he met a chap on the train who was working at the same factory as him. His name was Hugh Campbell and he lived around the corner from us in Binstead.

We also met two other families at this time, the Firth Family, Kath and her partner Terry and their kids, all 7of them, what an amazing crowd they were. About the same time we met the Marden family, Colin and Joan and their 4 kids. We all had some wonderful times together.

My dad was a self-taught mechanic, which he obviously got from his father Tommy –this will become very relevant later on. Around this time he decided to finish working at the car factory in Oxford and concentrate on his life on the island bringing us all up. Things were getting better and better apart from school, which I hated but I needed to be there. We all had an amazing summer the school holidays were spent on the beach of course.

My dad was working as a mechanic during the day and as a bouncer in the evening at the local nightclubs.

After having a lovely Christmas and New Year it was time to look forward to 1968.I remember it was a cold winter even some snow at times which was quite unusual for the island. I was looking forward to the summer on the beach once again. I went with my dad exploring different things around the coast.

About a week after my 8th birthday in April I was messing around with my friend Gary Ockendon, we were trying to move big rocks when one came down and broke my hand and also chopped off the end of my finger on my right hand! There was a lot of blood pouring out all over the place and I, as you can imagine was in a lot of pain. We reached the nearest property Seagull Cottage, that is situated on Binstead beach next to Tatlers fishing club. When we reached there the two elderly ladies who lived there wrapped tea towels around my hand to try and stop the flow of blood. They then took us in the back of their black Standard 8 car to home.

Gary got out and my mum got in and the two ladies took us to Ryde Hospital to be fixed up. They took a skin graft from my left fore arm and grafted it onto the end of my finger I had lost before being sent home later that evening in a lot of pain. The only thing that was good about the accident was the fact that I got a couple of weeks off school! As the summer progressed I was mended and able to go back in the sea and carry on learning to swim. I enjoyed the beach and the seaside so much and started watching the cruise ships coming in and out of Southampton. I soon got to know them all and could name them from quite a distance away.

I knew at that point that one day I would be on those ships.

Later that summer dad was working on the doors at the Seagull Club. This club always had live groups performing. They were always at our house in Binstead, either before the show or after they would stay the night as there was no ferry back at that time. I remember the Tremolos and Simon Dupree of the Big Sound staying at our house. I think Procol Harum and the Dave Clarke five were also there. I remember having a pillow fight with Dave from the Tremelows. What an amazing life mine was turning out to be.

Around this time my mum and dad took me to see the Hippies at Afton near Freshwater for the pop concert. I remember it well, it was packed with something like half a million people. At the time there was rubbish and mud and even human sewage underfoot.

There was a traffic cop there that no-one liked he was very well known as being the most horrible person anyone has ever met. He always looked immaculate, with his highly polished helmet and boots and his bike was a showpiece. He always wore big pure white gloves. Well this day we were wondering around the muddy field when we saw a car that had got stuck in the water/sewage. It started spinning it's back wheels and right behind was this copper on his bike looking all bright and shiny. Not for long! he got covered from head to foot and at the same time there were hundreds of people watching this display, they were cheering and laughing as they knew how horrible he was. His name was PC Gurd and from that day onwards he became known as gurd the turd!

Everything seemed to be going very well when in 1969 my dad and several of his closest friends were arrested for burglary, charged and sent to prison in Winchester. We were all devastated but at least they were all together in the same prison. The only thing that bothered me was the fact that I was the only male in the house with three females. I used to visit Dad every couple of months until he was released in 1970.

When he came out we were back again searching the beaches. We were walking across Ryde Golf Course when we met an old chap called Alfie Eldridge who was searching for golf balls that had been lost in the trees and hedges and the long grass. Alfie was an amazing character, I remember him with his dirty old hankie taking snuff every few minutes. We saw an opportunity here and also started looking for golf balls. I made a few pounds from this and so continued to do this for about 18 months.

My dad went into business with a chap called Freddie Fox around this time. He was a tree specialist, I can see him now sawing down huge trees and making sure they landed correctly some of them were just a few feet away from the respective properties.

It was also around this time we started collecting old Victorian bottles which was becoming quite the thing to do. We got several families involved and would search everywhere. Not only would we look for Victorian bottles which are very valuable but also old stone ginger beer bottles. Anything else we dug up, we were selling to bottle dealers that were popping up all over the country. Our own bottle dealer was called Keith Shutter. I can recall 60 or 70 bottle collectors; most of them were from Binstead. Most things we did everyone got involved. I can remember Dennis Firth and his brother Peter and step dad Terry digging up some amazing bottles at Oak Field between the recreation ground football ground and the railway line at St John's Station in Ryde. Other tips that we were digging at the same time down Perowne Way in Sandown and America Wood Shanklin. The other ones were Pottery Shoot in Haylands and a good tip in Whippingham. Being an island we could specialise in just Isle of Wight stuff to collect. We specialised in Ginger beer bottles whereas some people collected other beer bottles or other types of bottles

In 1971 my dad introduced car banger racing at Thorness Bay Caravan Park. It was owned at that time by one of his friends Fred Sage. They had racing there every two weeks and hundreds of spectators. This is where I learnt to drive between 11 and 12 years of age. The races were brilliant and I remember there were great crashes on the circuit as well.

My dad came up with the idea that whoever does the fastest lap of the track at Thorness Bay, taking into account that this track had 2 chicanes and 2 sharp bends that also dipped suddenly downhill with crash barriers all around. Everyone was after the track record, quite a few people tried with their own cars; they all wanted the large silver trophy. Week after week the time kept coming down.

One chap in particular, Arthur John Williams, who had been born and bred on the island, tried many times in his racing car and also in his friend's car. He failed on so many occasions we thought he had given up.

However, after a few days he decided to go to Binstead Garage. At the time they were Volkswagen dealers. He went in pretending that he wanted to buy the new VW Beetle but needed to take it out for a test run first. They allowed him to do this and he drove out of the garage and turned up at the racetrack in his brand new white VW Beetle.

He said to everyone "Now I will win the trophy for the fastest lap on the track" Sure enough, after a few warm up laps, slipping and sliding around in the mud as it was a grass and mud track he set off. After spinning the wheels on that car, almost coming to grief into the crash barriers and the trees and also nearly rolling it over several times he did smash the record. He then took the car and gave it a thorough wash and took it back to the garage. He told them it was quite a good car and that he would give it a lot of thought. Of course he never went back, I just pity the person who bought that car after him!

The following weekend was a race day, no one came close to beating the record so John was awarded his trophy in front of several thousand spectators, and all unaware of how he had done it.

I tried a couple of times, in two different cars. I was only around 12 at this point; unfortunately I rolled one of the cars over and completely wrote it off. It was a Morris Minor with built in role cage. I then got another one that I think I paid £20 for, again it was all done up for racing, no windows or light and a built in roll bar. It was a bit wet that day on the mud and grass I took a sharp right hand bend and slid into the corner. As I spun the car around I completely ripped the back end off. I decided then that I couldn't keep buying cars; I would let John keep his trophy for the fastest lap.

Later that year I was down on the golf course with Archie still looking for golf balls and listening to all his stories of his earlier life. One of these was about him picking winkles on the beach and send sackfuls of them to Billingsgate fish market in London. What had brought this fact to mind was the day before he had seen an advert in the local paper from a chap in Portsmouth called Jerry Glover who was a shellfish dealer in Portsmouth. Of course Alfie and I went to the beach at low tide to see whether it was a viable thing to do. When I got home I rang Jerry Glover and he said "Well lad, if you want to pick winkles for me I will come over to the Island every Sunday, do my rounds and pick them up from your address" So, off we went, bucket and hessian sacks and our Wellington boots. No-one, apart from my parents and Alfies family knew what we were up to, we were making money! This carried on until the March or April 1972. The weather was getting warmer so the season finished and would reopen in the September.

That summer was great and then it struck me that I could turn this winkle picking into a business. I spoke to Jerry saying I could save him a lot of time if I was allowed to get my school friends to help collect the winkles from his customers that he had all around the island. I could pay them at the correct rate that he would fix but of course I had to have a decent price from him as I was saving him a lot of time and energy. He agreed with me thinking it was an excellent idea and agreed he would pick up from me every Sunday at my house in Binstead. He thought it was a very clever idea; he could come over with his lorry pick them up, take them away to be exported to France and Spain.

In the September my dad got involved, driving us all to the beaches. We were earning lots of money, more than my school teachers were. I had about 30 school kids working with me as well as 15 or

20 adults some of whom were our good friends the Firth, Marden and Long families and of course our good friend Alfie.

I remember the first year of dealing in winkles where we had sent off some 75tons of them. It was incredible, we got them from the following: - Seaview, Binstead, Newtown, Porchfield, Allum Bay, Freshwater Bay, Bembridge Ledge, St Helens and the river Medina and of course my favourite picking ground of Woodside Bay and Kings Key.

1972 or thereabouts in thick fog one of the large passenger ferries called MV Shanklin from Portsmouth to Ryde Pier, when negotiating it's approach to avoid the pier sliced through the pier. It was the road part of the pier and this damaged the tram part of it as well. Shortly after this happened a taxi, a black Ford Zephyr I seem to remember, travelled up the pier and fell into the hole. The car, the driver and the passenger were rescued though. The only way to get to the end of the pier to catch a ferry then was to take the train, which hadn't been affected by the crash. The hole in question was about 25 foot wide by 60 feet long. If you looked at it from the beach when the tide was out there were metal pylons, wood and all sorts of stuff that made the scene look very dangerous. I thought at the time how lucky the people in the taxi were to get out unharmed.

There were dozens of cars stranded on the end of the pier with no way of getting back to land. After approximately a week a car ferry was sent and each car was loaded, then sent to Fishbourne car ferry terminal where they were reunited with their owners. After this the pier was closed for quite a long time, the ferry itself was not too badly damaged.

Later this year there had been a collision in the English Channel between two tankers carrying crude oil. One of them managed to get to its destination, unfortunately the other one that was called the Pacific Glory was beached at Sandown Bay. It caught fire and hundreds of tons of crude oil escaped into the sea. I can remember the thick black plumes of smoke rising from the ship for days and saw the oil spewing out into the sea, which of course was burning. I can't be sure how many people lost their lives on that fateful night. I know there were quite a few. It was then a race against time to save the beaches from the awful crude oil that had also started taking its toll on the sea birds and other marine life.

As the nights went past the authorities were out there with fireboats spraying water onto the fire whilst tugboats were trying to put out the fire by spraying detergent on the oil as it was still spewing out of the Pacific Glory. A couple of nights later the wind picked up to gale force and the seas became very rough around the stricken tanker. Added to this one of the tugboats called the Harry Sharman had dragged its anchor and was swept under the cliff at Culver. It was a large tugboat and as it hit the beach it had holes from landing on the rocks and subsequently filled up with water every time the tide came in. I remember for days after that all the experts from the marine and safety organisations were trying to find a way of getting all the equipment and cleaning barrels of detergents off the deck, before it all ended up on the beach.

Nothing seemed to happen for a couple of days no-one had been on the tugboat so one afternoon as my dad and some of his friends and me of course were walking along the beach at low tide we got on board and had some photos taken. This tugboat had started to become a wreck and whilst we could still have the stuff off it we took the mouthpiece that sent messages down to the engine room, which was made of solid brass. We also took other pieces of brass and the ship's telegraph that is now residing in a pub in London!

The experts finally decided to pour concrete into the hole but that didn't work as when they tried to tow the boat off the rocks the pressure of the water just pushed it further out. That was the end of it.

A month or two went by and we were on the beach again to see the Harry Sharman. A chap came running along asking where the nearest phone box was. He said his mate was drowning out on the wreck. We were only kids but had my dad with us and sure enough, this chap with his brand new diving equipment was on the boat. We put him over a rock and started to pump the water out of him but unfortunately it was too late. The man had been sick in his mask and we also found out later that he had never been diving alone in the sea before. What a sad and tragic loss.

Nowadays at low tide you can see at the Harry Sharman protruding from the water at Culver.

After we had finished our Winkle picking season in 1972 my dad and his mate Colin Marden were really getting into the sport of water skiing, so, at every opportunity I would go and sit in the boat whilst my dad was towing Colin or Colin was towing my dad on the skis. I did have a couple of goes myself but was not very good at it at the time.

Later that summer I had a call from someone called Phil Hammond who informed me that he was a shell fish merchant and that he had purchased the winkle business round from Jerry Glover who had gone on to do other things. A week or so later Phil Hammond came over to visit my parents and myself in Binstead to sort out further business involving the winkles. Apparently he owned a large shellfish business in Portsmouth with lots of fishing and shellfish boats unloading their catches to him. After a good chat we decided that all was well and we would carry on with the winkles, so it was winkle-picking season 1973

All my pickers were itching to get out onto the beaches to start earning all their money again. Phil Hammond came over to pick the first lot up; we had amassed about six or seven tons over the first 10 days. He was paying a good price so I was making a lot of profit plus the money that I had for any I had picked.

Phil then asked whether we ever found any oysters on the beach to which we said "Yes, we can get loads", so whilst my other friends were picking winkles, a great friend of mine, Hilding Eklund and my self started picking oysters. Phil came over the following week; we had a few tons of winkles and over half a ton of oysters. He really could not believe the quality of the oysters that we were finding on our local beach.

At that point I was paying £13 per hundredweight and I was getting £17 so making £4, which was a very good profit in those days. The oysters were fetching £32 a hundredweight and that really boosted the money up.

Later that year we started picking up clams as well but the only person buying clams at that time was a chap called Cyril Lucas who owned Newtown Oyster Fishery. He was also a magistrate, he was a lovely chap so we decided to take some oysters and winkles with us and see what he thought. My dad stepped in and would take me over there to unload with one of the pickers. As we used to arrive Cyril would weigh up the winkles and the oysters and pay us accordingly, however the clams were something different, they had to be graded into small, medium and large. So, we would be on our knees picking out small that went into one basket, medium into another and the large into another. There were three different prices you see. The extra large clams were unable to be sold and so were thrown into the river in Newtown called clan making which incidentally has nothing to do with the Clan Fisheries. Those large clams I threw back into the river that day were to be a major part of my life 30 years down the line.

After Xmas 1973 I was getting all sorts of shellfish dealers phoning and turning up at our house trying to get us to sell to them as the stuff we had here was of far better quality than most places on the mainland.

That year I remember all the local kids bought brand new chopper bikes from a company in Newport where M&S now stands, these bikes cost £36 each I remember I had a blue one.

Life was amazing with better opportunities coming up all the time. We were naughty at times though. We would get up at 3 or 4am in the morning to pick winkles on the beach with torchlights. On the way there we would nip into the back of Island Bakeries and take a load of fairy cakes out of the back of the delivery vans that were being loaded. We had a great feast of these cakes on our way to the beach.

In the spring of 1974 we met a man called Ian Murray. He was a bottle collector also postcards and other historical items. Just by chance one day we found an old 1936 Morris 8 car in an old barn in Woodsford Road in Wootton and after negotiating a price with the owner, we got the old car running. I can always remember the number plate of this car-it was ADL300. That night we had to go and pick it up but as Ian couldn't drive at this time, although he was 12 years my senior, dad drove us out there but I drove back to Binstead I was only 13 years old at the time mind you I was nearly 14!

So, another shellfish season came to a close-it was time to get the speedboat ready for another summer on the water with my dad and his friend Colin. During this year I wasn't sure whether or not I wanted to ski although they got me to have a go a couple of times which I finally managed to get up on two skis and started to get used to the sport. I preferred to be on the boat towing them both. I enjoyed that the most. It was a good summer; I was really getting into the sport of powerboat racing, which was held August bank holiday Sunday every year. It had started in 1961 and I started going to it in 1967 and still go to this day. The boats are approximately 30-40 feet long, some monohull some catamaran in the race down to Torquay and back. The race is known as the Cowes Torquay Cowes Powerboat race.

Soon after the powerboat weekend it was almost time to get ready for the new winkle season approaching on the 15 th September. More and more buyers were contacting me from all over the country. There was a lot of shellfish coming off the island, it was such an amazing time and the money was still pouring in. All the local kids and their mothers and fathers like the Friths were doing very well at the winkle picking, we were also hitting the oysters hard and started to go elsewhere like Woodside, Kings Key, Bembridge Ledge, Porchfield and Newtown. We had a 2 mile trek if we wanted to go to the beach and another 1.1/2 to get to Newtown. We were loaded up with 50+ kilos of winkles or oysters in sacks on our backs, it did take a long time to get home.

One picker took a day, I can remember that were on our way to Porchfield and it started to snow, we carried on though. By the time we got to the beach after our trek, the wind was picking up, really cold. Whilst I was on the beach I noticed an oystercatcher had got stuck with some line around it. After picking all the shellfish and taking the seabird back home with us it took 7 hours. The snow was laid deep with drifts especially round the country lanes of Porchfield and Newtown.

After about two weeks of feeding the bird with live sprats and other fish we released it back into the wild that was lovely to see.

It was approaching Christmas 1974,I can remember us all having a lovely Christmas that year. All the lads came round for a can of beer with us to celebrate the Christmas break before going back to the beaches on 27th December

During this time in the 70's when the price of scrap metals was at an all time high my dad, Dave Long and I would be out and about collecting as much copper, brass and lead to sell to the local scrap metal dealer Jack Newbury, who used to live at Parklands Avenue in Ryde with his wife Doris and their three kids. Joy, was their daughter and in those days was a real tomboy with the blond hair. You could tell she idolised her dad Scrappy

Jack. Her dad used to call her bomber. We used to unload tons and tons of scrap metal and Jack and Bomber would bag it up in two sacks for each type of metal. This they would store in the garage until they had enough to take to the main scrap yard that belonged to Joe Valvono.

At this time there was a lot of silver coming to our house via dad's friends who were out robbing jewellers, churches and yacht clubs etc. Some of it was worth a fortune, there were huge silver trophies and of course scrap silver which went through my dad. Also there was quite a lot of gold. I remember my uncle Norman bringing lots of Krugerrands back from South Africa. One day there were at least 60 to 70 of them piled up on our coffee table at home.

There was also the time when a jeweller got robbed in Cowes and the police were everywhere and yet the guys who robbed it just jumped into my dad's boat which was only 40 m away and headed straight back round to Wootton and unloaded everything and got away with it. I also remember my dad feeding a police dog a mars bar which had a sleeping pill in it. The Headlines in the paper read he sleeps for three days. My dad and his friends were always one step ahead of the police apart from one occasion when they all ended up in prison because they were grassed up by someone called Mr Wilson but he got his comeuppance and I doubt if he ever grassed on anyone again. He was meddling with the wrong people. They sorted it.

I remember going out to the forts in the Solent and stripping them of all the copper, brass and lead with my dad and Dave Long. There was also huge electrical cables that fed St Helen's Fort running under the surface of the seabed and at low tide these were visible so we spent many nights down there cutting sections off, carrying it to shore then stripping off the armour around the cables. After this, the wax paper before burning all of the rubber coating. Once this was done we would put it in the sea to cool it down then brush it off with a yard broom to make it look nice and shiny as copper was fetching a very good price at that time. Out on the forts having stayed for a couple of nights at a time was great but quite spooky as they are quite big with all sorts of noises going on inside like dripping water, wind blowing, windows or doors creaking and of course the pigeons fluttering around. This continued for about a year until, they were stripped bare.

That year there was one night when my dad asked me to help him move some scrap. Late at night we went to Ryde cemetery where he had already dismantled a huge brass bell, this bell was known as a mourning bell. It was over 100 kg which we rolled from the cemetery to our old A40 car, we managed to get it in but by now it was approaching midnight so we drove across the golf course with it onto Binstead Beach where we buried it in the sand and left it for about 6 months. After a mega storm about 4months later I went down to the beach and there the bottom of the bell was sticking out of the surface of the sand. Luckily I was alone so I chucked loads of seaweed and driftwood over it so no-on would notice and went home to tell my dad. We went down and spent a few hours just in case anyone had seen anything and when it was dark we dug it up took it home and then the following day just after dark took it to Scrappy Jack and got a really good price for it as it did weigh 100kgs!

Scrappy jack died several years ago. On Amnesty Day 2018 Jack would have been 100 years old. Their eldest son Keith worked as a journalist and had a column in the Isle of Wight County press, he died a few years ago.

In 2017 Joy and I became a couple. We had some great times and some nice holidays, unfortunately in the late 2017 her mum became very ill and as she couldn't look after herself Joy went to help her. At the age of 94 she unfortunately died 1pm on Valentines day 2018. That left Joy and her younger brother Alan. I still see Joy occasionally and she seems to be doing okay. Alan is also doing okay with his garden clearing business and everything else he has done like skip hire. When Joy and I got together in 2017 I can remember taking her round to see my mum and dad. My dad at the time was suffering from Alzheimers. I said to him "Dad this is Joy the daughter of Scrappy Jack who used to buy all our scrap off us in the 70's Can you remember him?" "Yes, I remember

and he never cared where it came from either"
That was amazing and straightaway brought tears
to my eyes.

In August 1975 I bought my first house. It was
at 10 Harvey Close, East Cowes. I paid £15,500
for it. I bought it from my Auntie Pat and Auntie
Myrtle, who had moved to the island a few years
previous. As they had no families to leave the
house to it was a good idea that I gave them £1000
down and the rest was paid in August each year
until it was paid off. The agreement was that they
would live there for the rest of their lives and I
would take the house over when they had both
passed away. It was a fabulous opportunity as I
was able to afford it easily and had it paid off in
4 years.

I sold shares of that house to my uncle Norman
who lived in South Africa with his wife Ethne and
his children, Peter, Gill and Lloyd. Norman was
my dad's eldest brother, Auntie Pat and Auntie
Myrtle lived a good many years after I bought the
house. We spent money and time on modernising
the house before we sold it off.

I cannot believe other people don't do it the same as I did. Remember, I was only 15 years old at the time.

We had been working the Oysters and Winkles since the September as we got to Christmas I was thinking what an amazing year it had been.

In the autumn of 1975 I had a few more goes at water-skiing. I managed to do quite well and thought to myself, I could take this on.

After the Christmas break we went back to the beaches picking up shellfish. We found more places to go as well. Also by this time the bottle collecting had dwindled as most hobbies do from time to time, However, I started collecting again in a massive way in later years.

The winkles had risen to £23 per hundredweight, which was very good for those days, as the spring approached it was time to get the boat in the water for some more water skiing. For some very odd unknown reason I just got straight up and on with it, there was nothing that was going to make me fall off. I think all the walking on the beaches and carrying all the shellfish kept me very fit and healthy and that contributed to my doing well at water skiing.

During this time I was never at school, my official leaving day was May 23rd 1976

The shellfish picking had finished and I decided to start a water skiing school. The water skiing lanes meant we could come fast into the beaches at Woodside Bay where there was a Pontins Holiday Camp and also a Warners Holiday Camp which meant I already had a captive audience of around 2500 people a week from the people who were taking their holidays there.

Warners, who could see the potential for people coming on holiday, approached me as their site backed on to the beach where we were skiing. Within 2 weeks with my parents I was running our own business of water skiing at Warners Woodside Bay. I was actually living at the holiday camp, which was amazing.

I was getting very good at it and by this time I could ski on only one ski which meant I could go faster but it was more difficult to keep ones balance at times.

We were contacted by Jeff Jury from Medina Borough Council to ask if we could put on a show for the regatta at Ryde. We decided to start a challenge of water skiing round the Isle of Wight which had been done once before by a chap called Chris Turvey who had set a time of just over two hours although he did fall off once

The summer of 1976 was well and truly on us and every single day was very, very hot and sunny and the seas were quite calm. The council had put up posters all over the island about the regatta coming up at Ryde with my photo on them because of the water skiing challenges that were taking place. Although I felt very nervous with the thought of having to ski right around the island I also felt proud to be the main star of the attraction.

July 10th arrived, day of the Ryde Regatta and my attempt to water-ski all around the Isle of Wight.

All the timekeepers were ready at advantage points around the island so that I could be seen from shore at all times on my journey. I chose to go clockwise so that I could tackle the tide race (which is the point where two tides collide with each other) around Bembridge Ledge first followed by tide race off St Catherine's point. I knew I would be tired by the time I reached the Needles but I hoped I would be fine.

It was time to go, I was up on my ski 75 feet at the end of rope pulling me, which was driven by my dad. We went over the start line at about 35 to 40 miles an hour. It was a great run past Seaview, then Bembridge and across to Sandown Bay and down towards Saint Catherine's point. As I reached each one of these points I would put up one arm as that gave our timekeepers the sure knowledge that I was fine and they would then phone through to Radio Solent who in turn would put it out on the air that Trevor Towill the water skier had just past a certain vantage point. When we got to Saint Catherine's point there was a huge long swell coming in and a slight chop on top of that. We had to slow down and as the boat was going down one of the huge swells I was still coming up the other side so frequently lost sight of the boat. After some time I could see the Needles Lighthouse and I knew that once I got there and then back into the Solent, the seas would be a lot calmer for my final run to Ryde. As we rounded the Needles I raised my arm to let the lighthouse keeper know that I was okay, he gave us a blast on the foghorn before contacting Radio Solent as before.

After rounding the Needles as we got back into the Solent there were quite a few speedboats waiting for me to escort me and keep me going. I was feeling very tired as it was taking a lot longer that we had anticipated due to the high seas at the back of the island. As I came up through the Solent I was starting to feel quite good again as the sea was a lot calmer and all the boats were keeping me going. Then I could see Cowes and East Cowes and after coming around East Cowes point I could see Ryde Pier, I knew I didn't have long before I was home as we came around the end of Ryde Pier and up the Hovercraft channel towards the beach at my pavilion. I cross the finishing line after being on that ski for 2 hours 55 minutes and 30 seconds!

The thousands of people lined the Ryde seafront to cheer and greet me back. I had done it at just 16 years old! I had become the most junior person to water-ski around the island I also became the junior record holder for skiing around the island which was an amazing achievement. I was also the first person to water-ski around the island on one ski non stop.

As I came out of the water there were TV cameras, radio reporters and newspaper reporters and I felt so fantastic for what I had achieved and I knew then that it could only make my business better now that I had a couple of world records to my name.

After the Regatta we all trouped back to the Warners where we were greeted to a great reception by all the staff and lots of holiday makers as the radio broadcasts throughout the day was put through the tannoy system at the park. It was amazing to think so many people had been listening in to my progress.

The following day I was back to normal teaching people to water ski and also taking people on our boat rides around the bay. The weather in 1976 was so hot and sunny, I remember having long curly blond hair and an amazing suntan, everyone wanted to be in the sea, I was packed with customers wanting to learn. Due to the tides we were only able to work for 6 hours a day. This weather went on for two and a half months and as the water skiing season came to a close it was back to the beaches to pick winkles and oysters. I enjoyed this part of my life just as much as the water-skiing lessons.

About the end of October 76 the weather changed quite quickly and after the heat of the summer it became quite cold I recall by the middle of November we were getting lots of frost but regardless of this fact we were on the beaches 7 days a week.

On December 23rd we decided that we would take a week off until January 2nd or so and this became normal for the next few years. We had some quite nasty weather in January and February 1977 with some snowfall and very cold winds but it was doing the harvest of the winkles some good as these sort of conditions they like.

Around this time there had been a delivery to my dad of approximately 40 kg of silver ware which consisted of mainly knives, forks , spoons tea caddies tea sets but all solid silver. This was very hot and was definitely being looked for so after dark my dad and I went down to Ryde Pier and buried it about 4 foot down in the sand and there it stayed for about a year before we dug it up again.

By the early spring I was itching to get back on the water and start skiing again but I knew I still had a few weeks on the beaches before moving back to Warners at the end of April. It soon came round and sure enough with a brand new powerboat and engine it was time to ski again.

I remember the manager at the camp whose name was Roy Burke couldn't believe how full the holiday camp was for the summer this was all due to the watersports they had to offer and the amount of advertising that I got through TV, radio and newspapers the previous year.

Summer 1977 was great. I was able to do lots of skiing and trying to make my second attempt for another world record by skiing around the island. On 15th September 77, which was also the first day of the winkle picking season, was the day as the weather was favourable, to have another go at skiing around the island.

On 15th September 1977 was time to go for another attempt so after knowing that all the timekeepers were in position around the island it was time to set off. I decided this time to go anti clockwise just to see if it was an easier route and to get the tide race at the Needles over and done with first and also the wash off the ferries crossing the Solent. So, we set off at about 40 miles an hour, heading straight down the Solent towards the Needles hitting a few washes from shipping and ferries that slowed us down slightly but we didn't have much difficulty with that.

Once we reached Yarmouth we had made good time and could see the Needles ahead and as before I raised one arm to let the timekeepers know I was okay. My dad was driving the boat with my friend Eric Eklund acting as navigator to let my dad know any signs that I made. Light speed up or slow down and let me know how we were doing. After giving the lighthouse keeper a wave as I went past we were then on our way to St Catherine's Point and it was lovely to see the English Channel was calm. As we reached Saint Catherine's it became quite rough as the two tides meet so for a couple of miles we had to slow down as it would have been difficult to get back up on my ski in those conditions had I have fallen off. We made it through and got the speed back up again and rounded Ventnor and Bonchurch before heading across Sandown Bay towards Culver. At this point disaster struck as a piece of rope got entangled around our propeller and the boat had to stop. This took 12 minutes to fix and by the time the rope had been cleared and I was back on my ski and we continued we were back in the Solent coming over Bembridge Ledge and up towards Seaview I could see Ryde Pier, which was a great sight and I knew we could still get the record. We went flat out across Ryde Sands and over the finishing lines at a few seconds after 2 hours and 10 minutes and yes I had smashed the junior record. Even though if we had not got tangled up in that rope I would have crossed the line about two minutes under 2 hours but it wasn't to be so I knew I would have to do it again in 1978. The skiing season was over; it was time to hit the shellfish again.

Also during September we went across to Southampton Boat Show to have a look at the new powerboats, as we wanted to order one for our 1978 season at the holiday camp.

By this time I was getting some sponsors, we got the most amazing deal from Welsh Powerboats Ltd that were based in Milford Haven in Wales. The boat we chose was a 16-foot mirage powerboat and we were to have the actual one that was at the Boat Show. The company put a sign saying sold to " Trevor Towill Isle of Wight Water ski Champion and holder of three world records as the youngest person to ski around the Isle of Wight, the fastest junior to ski around the Isle of Wight and the only person to have skied around the Isle of Wight non-stop".

It was just amazing to see my name on the boat at the boat show. About a week later we had to go to Southampton to bring our new boat home, we then took it over to Bembridge outboards to have a brand new 80hp Mercury outboard engine fitted. This was going to be a very quick boat but first of all we had a winter full of shellfish to sort out and collect so it was time to knuckle down and start work again on the beaches right through until Christmas where we had our usual week off and started again on the beaches just after NewYear. 1977 had been a very lucrative year with amazing things happening I remember the year ending in style with a great Christmas and New Year and now to welcome in 1978

Over the last few years I had a few girlfriends but nothing really serious as I was concentrating so much on my work. During the summer months whilst at Warners I had more of a social life and was lucky enough to have a good choice of girls. The holiday camp was full up every week and I made many friends and taught many people to Ski. Change over was always on a Saturday so each and every Friday night the entertainments team would be called out onto the stage I was included in this as well as everyone who had done well at the water skiing were handed a certificate of competence to water-ski a certain distance, which was signed and dated by me. Some of the people came back two or three times in the season as they loved it so much which I felt was wonderful. There was a girl on reception called Cheryl Palmer from Essex who later became Cheryl O'Connor who used to write on the reception board messages from people who had phoned to rebook for water-skiing and send regards to Trevor the instructor. She also received quite a lot of mail for me. Cheryl loved to come out in our boat during her lunch break as she loved to be around my family and I. Funnily enough, years later having lost touch with Cheryl she tracked me down on Facebook and she and her husband came to see me again on the island a few times

In July 1978 we put on another show for Ryde Regatta. We actually had a 50mile race in the Solent and in that we had 16 boats and skiers enter. I came second and again the local council had put posters of me that felt good. At the end of the summer the holiday camp was coming to a close it was time to do a practice run ready for the race again to water-ski around the island. With the weather favouring the 17th September it was a case of training constantly for a few days doing 25 miles flat out.

The next thing that happened was that all of a sudden I went up in the air and landed upside down in the water behind the boat. What had happened I was 74foot behind the boat with a 12-foot shark that had come up behind it. I ended up in the water very close to it. Luckily for me it wasn't a Maneater just a Porbeadle but it made me get back onto the ski very quickly.

The 17th September arrived and at 9am I flew across the start line going anti clockwise again on a lovely calm morning. All the timekeeper were in place and this day all went well, I finished without any mishaps and I had smashed the senior record as I was now 18 years of age and a classed as a senior with a time of 1 hour 51minutes and 30 seconds which gave me every single record there was and two of those records were world records. What a feeling that was but what a huge comedown when the following day it was time to go on the beaches picking shellfish for another six months.

Leading up to Christmas 1978 me and a couple of my mates also got work at Warners painting the chalets for the following season. The idea was when the tide was in we would be painting and when it went out we would be on the beach picking shellfish. We carried on until our usual Christmas week off which by this time we were all looking forward to. After the usual fabulous Christmas and New Year we had lots of plans and things to do for 1979

At the beginning of 1979 I looked forward to the year ahead and what it might produce. but first we had to get through another shellfish season. This year though, I had a chance to go dredging on one of the local trawlers owned by Colin Babington. I think it was March of that year I went on his boat to catch oysters, I remember absolutely loving it as I had always wondered what was on the bottom of our Solent. For some unknown reason early that year before the summer season started there was so much shellfish around and the prices stayed up as in the past years as the Scottish and Irish winkles came onto the market in Spain and France the prices would go down slightly. This obviously meant that the Spaniards and French were eating a lot of seafood.

In the middle of April it was time to move back to Warners and start the summer season. The boat we used was looking particularly good; it was very fast and looked amazing in the water. It looked like it would be a very busy season. In the June we had our first water-ski championship race. I was about 30 miles around the circuit and I was running second for about 1.1/2 laps before passing the leading boat. I carried on to win that race and received the Linda Howarth trophy. I should point out that Linda was one of the dancers at Warners who was great fun to be around as she was always giggling so we decided to name a trophy after her. Later that day it was race number 2 I had an amazing start but was feeling tired so had to slow down, I stayed third for a couple more laps then I realised that there was only about 5 or 6 miles to go to the finish so I signalled to the driver and the navigator to speed up. I then managed to pass the two boats on the last leg and cross the line to win the Warner Holidays Trophy. After that I definitely had something wrong with me, I slept for hours after those two races.

In the July I started dating one of the greencoats she was a dancer named Paula Semple. We got on so well as a couple and stayed together for about 5 years before her dancing career took her over to Japan and other places for about a year. That meant our relationship would fizzle out although today Paula is married with 4 children and is still a good friend of mine and lives on the island. She originated from Leicester to work at Warners and I can remember going to stay with her parents when we got time off. I always remember her address as 99 Mere Road Wigdon Magna Leics !

That summer our next race was Ryde Regatta and another circuit race of about 30 miles. The seafront was packed and we had about 16 or 17 boats taking place in this race. As we were doing our laps the leg out to sea was quite rough. This meant I had to hold on as best I could, after the start I was about 5th so I knew I had my work cut out I was passing the other boats one by one. At the finish I managed to pass the leading boat that was towing Chris Turvey. Because of the conditions offshore some of the boats had damage including ours, which had a broken seat and a split windscreen. The rest of the summer season was busy, we had a race in Yarmouth where I came second and a race where I came first and then two races in Sandown where I got a first and a second that made me the Water-skiing champion 1979. I carried on teaching people to ski until the end of that season before going back to the winkles, oysters and clams until 1st November then I went back onto the trawler with Colin.

Paula and I were doing great, we were both living at my parents house and she would also come down to the beaches with me to help out.

Yet again we had our usual week off over Christmas and New Year and all of us had a great time and made our plans for 1980

1980 dawned very cold with outbreaks of snow but we carried on our shellfish season without much difficulty and by this time we were sending all our shellfish to a bloke called John Arrow. He was based in Selsey I remember. This winter had given us a very good harvest of shellfish and the prices were kept high.

On 2nd May my sister Sue and her husband Mike Harding had their first child, a boy, called Benjamin Michael, he was my first nephew so good reason to celebrate.

In 1980 the police were always turning over our house but we were quite clever and always one step ahead of them. We had loads of silver consisting of Albert chains and lots of silver teasets and lots of tea services, also gold sovereigns and krugerrands. There were also quite a few paintings. It had all been taken from a place in Ryde. I can remember that being buried in a field down by the railway line. I knew exactly where everything was in case anything happened to my dad. I could go and retrieve it if necessary. I am sure the police thought I was not very bright.

During early summer we decided to invest in a couple of parachutes to enable us to take people out parasending. This involved fixing the parachute to the boat and people could then get up to a height of 500 feet out of the water. As soon as we set them up in the morning we were fully booked for the day that proved to be really popular with the holidaymakers.

That summer I managed to win most of the races again for the third year running. It also made me the Isle of Wight water ski champion yet again.

Later that summer I bought my first fishing trawler, that I turned it into an oyster catching boat which meant putting a couple of winches on it and a gantry with a table either side of the boat to empty the catch out of the dredges that we were towing. It took me about 6 weeks to get it up and ready for oyster fishing on November 1st. A new government body calling themselves Southern Sea Fishery District, based in Poole Dorset, so typical government led. New rules meant that that we could only go out to catch oysters between 8am and 4pm Monday to Friday. This meant we were down about 40 hours a week on what we usually worked. They had petrol boats and they were out most days checking on us and our catch. We had to make sure that we had no undersized oysters on board. They gave us circular rings with a handle that you could lay the oyster on the ring flat and if it went through the ring it was undersized and had to be put back in the sea. The minimum oyster size we could take at that time was 2.1/2 inches but it still turned out to be very productive season with a good price of £1500 per ton.

Although I was now working out on the fishing trawler for oysters I was still buying loads of winkles, oysters and clams off the beach from my gang of pickers. I remember finishing work on 23rd December and knew that I wouldn't be going back until 3rd January. It felt good to be having some time off, 1980 had been a very good year and we were quite pleased with everything that we had achieved.

Between Christmas and New Year I slipped and broke my ankle, which really stopped me doing very much at all. I knew I had to get it mended properly otherwise my water-skiing days would be over so I was laid up and the crew had to take the trawler out to catch the oysters in the New Year

1981 Dawned with me laid up, my ankle still in plaster, all I could do was sort out the books and pay wages. I was not happy at all. Plenty of winkles were being picked and the trawler was out catching oysters.

About February the plaster was taken off and I then began the long journey back to full health. I had to be ready for the summer season. In the March I went out with Steve Harris who I had taught to water-ski, we did a lot together. On that first occasion I remember a lot of pain in my ankle after a couple of miles, I knew then I had a lot of work to do to get fit again. I desperately wanted to keep my Championship title going and I knew it wouldn't be easy. What followed was my going out as much as possible, coping with the pain to build up the muscles in my leg after being out of action for so long. I started teaching people to ski as well.

The shellfish season finished, another success with prices quite high so everyone was satisfied. My ankle was getting better daily and I was feeling more confident about the racing season coming up.

I think it was in the July 81 that a small ship or coaster was involved in a collision and was pulled into Sandown Bay where it was upside down. Although Sandown Bay is quite a distance from Woodside Bay we decided to start taking powerboat rides around to the stricken vessel. It was called the Tarpenpek. Our smaller boat concentrated on teaching people to ski whilst it became very popular for others to see the upside down boat. Mind you we did have a great trip back where they were able to see Culver and Bembridge lifeboat station, then back to Ryde before hitting Woodside Bay.

About four or five weeks later they took the ship away so the larger powerboat could carry on with it's role of towing the parachute and taking powerboat rides.

During that summer the son of Warner Brothers came to the camp to learn the trade of running a holiday camp. He would eventually move up the ladder and become one of the main people in charge of Warners Holiday Camps. I liked him, we got on really well and of course I taught him to ski. He used to come down to the beach every lunchtime. He would try and perfect his skiing. One day he decided to have a go, he was learning to ski on one ski, took off from the beach, of course everyone cheered and he looked back and crashed into a marker boy and broke his big toe! Henry was his name he limped back up the beach to rousing cheers. After a couple of weeks he was back we had a great season with him. However that summer seemed to pass really quickly.

Autumn then winter came and even the seaweed was freezing especially when we were working down there early in the morning as we could feel it crunching under our feet. The 23rd December came around and after being out in atrocious weather it was very welcome the week to ten days we were about to take off

At the beginning of 82 was still very cold, with very high winds and lots of snow. Somehow we managed to see the month of January through, never missing a day on the beach. In the February our new powerboat arrived. I couldn't wait to get the engine started by running it on the Solent. We were hoping for some better weather very high winds and very cold.

However on the morning of the 9th March on the news was the fact that a small 7000 ton coaster got into difficulties in the Channel and all her cargo which was iron fillings had shifted which meant that it was laying at 45 % to the starboard side. It was called the Gloriosa and was being carefully watched by the Coast Guard. It was decided to get the ship into the sheltered waters of the Solent so they decided to run the ship aground at Kings quay very near to Woodside Bay. I have very vivid memories of watching her come up the Solent as we were picking winkles that afternoon. I saw the crew on board and went to introduce myself to them all only to be told that the generator had blown up and because of this they had no electricity on board at all. They also asked where they could get food and provisions. I decided the best way was to wait until we had finished work and then we would take them off the ship in their rib, do their shopping and then drop them back at the beach. They could then make their way back to the ship in their rib. The ships captain was a German, Enrick West Hyder, his wife Heather came from Cornwall. Apart from there was a 1st mate and two Filipino crew and a Jack Russell dog. They were short of money so I spoke to the captain and he had the rest of the crew on the beach with us picking winkles. The following day I spoke to local TV and newspapers in an effort to get some clothing and food donated. All this was given to me and my winkle pickers to carry out at low tide. After a couple of days they had so much food but no electricity. At least they had gas for cooking and heating as we had provided them with some gas bottles through donations. They were very grateful for the generosity of local people, none of the local authorities wanted to know as usual. Once again it was down to me and my crew to carry on helping.

After about 6 or 7 weeks the shellfish season finished and we were back in Warners for the season. It was a lot easier going out in the powerboat than walking at low tide.

The TV companies were very interested in the story and we were giving lots of interviews as by this time. I was getting quite well known with people trying to help. However, the authorities were still absent. I got in touch with the owner of Warners, spoke to Bill Warner and asked if we could bring the crew ashore so that they could have a bath and be sat with us in the main dining hall? He straightaway said yes knowing how much publicity this would get for the camp. So, everyday we would launch the powerboat out to the Gloriosa, bring the crew back where they could bathe and eat with us in the dining room. It was lovely to see them so happy although the 2 Filipino crew didn't have visa we made sure that we got special clearance for them so that they could come ashore and enjoy the facilities of Warner's.

At this point a couple of friends of mine Malcolm and Graham decided to get some donations so that they could get a replacement engine to run the Gloriosa.

As I was teaching at the time I couldn't help with this but what I did I used to take people around the Gloriosa in the powerboat, so many people had seen the stricken vessel on the news.

Meantime, Malcolm and Graham had found an engine in an old lorry at the scrap yard. They purchased it and we all helped build a raft to take it out to the ship. Mark Rayment of Solent and Wight lines cruises brought his boat around from Cowes to tow the raft with the engine on out to the Gloriosa. Also on my mates boat called the Jenni Lee were BBC reporters taking lots of films of what was going on. They used one of the ships derricks to haul the precious engine onto the deck. We were still transporting the crew every day; sometimes they would even stay for the shows and have a beer or two.

After a couple more weeks Malcolm and Graham had successfully got the engine up and running and it was fantastic to see the Gloriosa lit up at night.

It was the first week of August; it was Cowes week with all yachts and everything going on at the famous Regatta. One lunchtime on the Friday of that week when a phone call came through from Bill Warner himself asking for David, my windsurfing instructor and myself. All the staff were running around like headless chickens wondering why we had been called to reception for the phone call. We were soaking wet as we were working and we all stood around, all the managers agog, desperate to find out what was going on. The phone rang and it was passed to me. The chap on the other end said who he was and wanted to thank David and I for what we had done and is still doing for the company. The amount of advertising you have generated from your water ski racing and also the stricken ship. I calmly said that's ok Bill that is what we are here for. Well the looks I got from the managers when I called him Bill, not Sir or Mr Warner were unbelievable. He then said what were we doing later that evening and I said not a lot this evening. So he then said well, if you can get yourselves down to Cowes I will send a special launch to pick you up at the marina as my family and I would love to have you onboard our yacht, Witchazel for food and drinks and to watch the fireworks.

Well, we couldn't believe it and nor could the management of the camp.

So that evening we went to Cowes and sure enough there was the launch which took us out to a huge yacht, it must have been 60 or 70 foot long. It had about 40 people onboard at the party and everyone one of them were firing questions at us asking all about the water skiing how did I come up with that idea etc and couldn't thank me enough for all the advertising and all that I had arranged for the Gloriosa. I remember leaving the yacht and being taken back to shore at about 1am. The following day there were so many questions from the managers, asking about Bill Warner as apparently no-one had ever been invited from any of the holiday camp staff for social occasions.

Back to work we went, back to normality, picking up the crew and enjoying the beautiful weather. I was the water-skiing champion again for 1982, in fact I won most of the ski races that year.

At the end of October it was back to the shellfish collections. I was still ferrying provisions every day to the Gloriosa as the camp had closed. We had organised another ship to off load the cargo of the Gloriosa so that any repairs could be done. We also organised fuel, diesel to be taken out so that it could steam away under it's own power to a secret location in Spain. I went back onboard for the last time with some of our winkle pickers and friends to have food and drink with them all before saying our goodbyes. I remember being on the beach at Woodside as she sailed away and being in tears as I had made some good friends and we had had some experiences. I was going to miss them all.

The following day was time to go out on the Oyster fishing boat and when we rounded into Woodside Bay it seemed so empty. All the other boat owners were saying what had happened to her? All I could say was she had to go as the authorities didn't give a damn about her. I knew exactly where she was heading-to a scrapyard in Spain. Graham Barnes sailed with her down to Spain then flew back home-the trip there took about 5 days.

So it was carry on with the shellfish through the first half of the winter up to Christmas when it was time for our usual 10 days off and start afresh in 1983

I decided in 1983 to leave the clams in Newtown Creek alone as the supply had diminished somewhat. In the January the weather was quite bad, very cold with snow at times and quite windy. This was quite a decision but I wanted to concentrate more on the oysters and winkles. At this point we were involved with a company in Portsmouth called Viviers. Uk. It was very handy as their premises were next to the Portsmouth Car ferry terminal, sometimes we could get off the ferry, unload our shellfish and catch the same ferry back home. We did these trips three or 4 times a week and usually carrying a ton of shellfish at a time.

Back to Warners once the season had finished teaching people to waterski and take powerboat trips around Woodside Bay. This summer we also used our fishing trawler to take people on mackeral fishing trips. At certain times we caught hundreds of mackerel so the holiday camp chef would take them from us and put them on the menu for dinner that evening. Some evenings, we would cook them on the beach and I ended up catering for a lot of people. I would sometimes smoke the mackerel by cutting them and filleting them, and then I would get a large metal grill and some concrete blocks. I would stand the concrete blocks up on the side to make a large square, putting the grill on top. I would put a load of oak sawdust under the grill, light it and let it smoulder. I would then put a large box over the top of the whole lot. In approximately half an hour we had the most beautiful tasting naturally smoked mackerel. The people loved it and within a short while we were sorting the fish out by the ballroom. Free snacks with a beer!

Suzuki racing was sponsoring me at the time I had to do a publicity stunt for them. The new boat was all done out in Suzuki racing colours with a huge Suzuki S on the front of it. I still had my race number Number 17 ,which had been with me since I started water-skiing racing. It had also been on all of my previous powerboats. The venue was Lakeside, which is at Wootton Bridge. It was quite shallow there but I was able to put on a good show, loads of cars were stopping on the bridge to watch what was going on, I remember thinking that bridge is getting quite close as the lake is not very big but I managed it, it was a great success.

1983 I had won the Isle of Wight water-skiing championship, I got a second at Yarmouth regatta, two firsts at Shanklin regatta and a first and 3rd at Sandown regatta.

After the summer season it was straight back to the seafood, again the prices were quite high. During the winter I started fishing with a very good friend of mine called Bert Sims, he was an amazing man who taught me a lot about fishing and sewing up fishing nets, we would row out to Ryde Beach with our nets, we tied one end of the net onto Ryde beach. The net would be about half a mile long with floats on the top and lead line on the bottom. We would be sat there 100 m off Ryde beach in the dark with sandwiches and coffee for about half an hour before picking up the nets again. We always had lots of grey mullet and sea bass and occasionally sea trout. After we had completed this we would go to the other side of the pier and do the same all over again. We had hotels that were interested in the sea bass and we sold all the mullet to the Indian stallholders on the street markets. In Newport, Ryde and Sandown some days we were selling around 200kg at 70p per kilo. The sea bass was fetching about £5 per kilo and we were getting about 10kilos per night.

Unfortunately Bert died a few years back but I remember so well this carried on for several years between catching oysters and winkles at low tide this was done on the incoming tide. We certainly had some amazing times out there sitting in the dark 100 m off Ryde beach

In the November I would be back on the oyster fishing trawler until Christmas. All the others were busy picking winkles for me. I became an agent for Viviers UK for buying the oysters from the 18 oyster fishing boats who fished off the island.

What made it easier was that all the boats came in to East Cowes marina at the same time as we were only allowed to fish 8am to 4pm Monday to Friday and because I was the oyster license holder which meant I had to be on board the boat my mum and dad took over from me, bought the oysters and delivered them every night by lorry to Viviers uk which was good. We were getting £150 cash for every ton we delivered to them.

It was now December 23 rd and time for a break as always it was a good Christmas and I had time to heal all the cuts and bruises we had sustained on the boat or on the beach.

1984 started as usual, we picked winkles and this went on until the middle of April. We were also out on the boat catching oysters at this time. The weather that year was very cold and damp with lots of fog, which never seemed to let up. I met a chap who worked as a lorry driver for Gateway Supermarkets on the island. He lived in Bristol at the time but decided after a few weeks to move to the island to live. His name was Alan Holmes and he was very eager to learn to water ski. He was getting on quite well, the camp was full every week, I was teaching lots of people to ski, lots of power boat trips and lots of people wanting to go mackerel fishing on the trawler. Alan on the other hand wanted to learn to ski on one ski but the difficulty was that he couldn't swim, which meant if he came off the skis we had to get to him pretty damned quick before something really nasty happened to him. This became quite the joke as people wanted to see him ski but couldn't swim. It is difficult to wear a life jacket as it becomes very cumbersome. Alan decided to buy himself a wet suit that helped keep him afloat!

That summer I remember had plenty of sunshine and lots of girlfriends that definitely made the job so much more worthwhile. In the evenings we used to sit near the beach in our cars and have our CB radios on, chatting to people all around the country. We all have CB names and mine was Mono man. There were a crowd of girls at Lee on Solent and they would be flashing their light at us whilst talking to them on the radio. They couldn't believe that they were talking to me as they had seen me on the TV. Of course this made me feel really good. They ended up coming over and staying at the camp a few times, things seemed to be easier in those days, and we had a lot of fun.

During August we had 50 soldiers to teach who came over from Pirbright in Surrey for the day. They turned up in their lorries and all their camouflage gear. They were allowed to go to the dining room and have breakfast and lunch. They didn't have to decide who was going first as the sergeant would go you 1st you 2nd, 3rd 4th 5th and so on so that they knew exactly where they were in the line, they were an amazing group of chaps. Of course word got out and lots of girls turned up once they heard they were there. Whenever I was driving the boat I always had someone in the boat with me, I could actually pick and choose the girls in those days.

During the morning I taught the soldiers then in the afternoon I taught people from the camp so we ended up working over low tide. Usually we only work three hours either side of high tide.

Cowes week came round and on the Friday night we travelled to Cowes to see the fireworks and the Red Arrows Display Team. We had done it for years and I continue to this day. I remember going again to the International offshore Power Boat race on the August bank holiday. It is amazing to see these huge class one powerboats travelling at well over 100 miles per hour racing down to Torquay and back; these boats are 40 foot long and arrive on articulated lorries.

It wasn't long until we finished the skiing at the camp; it was getting near to October where we were picking winkles, then in the November we were out again on the trawler catching oysters. I remember a lot of bad weather that year that meant that we were thrown around a great deal but the oysters were plentiful and the prices were good. We had a very successful season that year taking us up to December 23rd where we had lots of food and drink and relaxed until 3rd January

In 1985 there had been a huge fire at Warners in the April, the whole of the ballroom, games rooms, bars and restaurant and swimming pool complex were totally destroyed which meant that there would be no water skiing there that year. This was a real blow and a huge setback as we had so many things planned for the summer season.

What we decided to do was to move over to Warners Yarmouth to teach the skiing. It was no way as good as Woodside because the prevailing south-westerly wind would catch the inshore waters at Yarmouth and made the sea quite choppy at times whereas at Woodside Bay it would be flat and calm. We did this for sometime but then it was decided to return to Woodside Bay, do a lot of advertising and get people to come down for lessons. We also started teaching European family students from Sweden, Denmark, Germany and France, this soon became very popular, we were teaching up to 60 or 70 students a day aged between 12 and 18 years old. They were great as they were so slim and able to get up on the skis. My mate Alan Holmes and I split the work between us, we made a good team and it worked out to be very successful.

During this year some very, very expensive china birds were stolen about 8 of them worth thousands of pounds even then. They could never be brought out of the ground where we buried them on Woodside Bay Beach. Even to this day they are too hot to handle but one day in the future

I will dig them up and then will see what to do with them.

Once the summer season had finished it was back to the winkle picking which is when I came up with the idea of poaching oysters through the night in September and October before the official season started on 1st November. I teemed up with a top oyster fisherman called Roger Downer. We would go out from East Cowes after dark, round to Osborne Bay and Woodside Bay. This started to earn a lot of money. We were joined by a couple of boats from the mainland and another one owned by a friend of mine, Hilton Matthews who came from Wootton Creek. It had proved to be very lucrative season as you can imagine as we had two months extra income.

I knew that the following year we would be poaching again I would have it all sewn up properly with hardly any risk of being caught by petrol boats that were patrolling the oyster grounds of the Solent waters.

1986 dawned and it was quite uncomfortable working on the beach. The winds were high, very cold, quite often it would snow but it only last a few months and we reached the summer months.

That year Alan and myself were doing the teaching. Rather than the students having to make a formal trip to Woodside Bay we found an ideal area of beach that was only ¾ mile from Ryde so the students could walk along the beach to Binstead as the tide was coming in and after we had taught them to ski they could make their way back as the tide was then going out.

For the Ryde Regatta that year we did a large water-ski ing and Para sending show, it had attracted thousands of people. I remember being up in the parachute about 400 feet behind the powerboat that was towing me and as we turned to come back along the seafront I was able to manoeuvre the parachute so that it was right over the crowds, I dropped to about 200 feet and then I let go of my hands and hung upside down in the harness. I could hear the screams as they thought I was going to fall out. It was deliberate.

During my life I have always been interested in escapology, especially the life of Houdini. I had seen a local chap who was still in the early stages of learning the craft by escaping from a straightjacket. He had put up a challenge for anyone who could beat his time of escaping from a British Regulation straightjacket.

So, me being me, I thought I would have a go at it. Steve Harris and I managed to track down a straightjacket and I was put into the said jacket. It was very hot and uncomfortable, heavy as well. There were 13 buckles going down the back and a very big buckle going under the crotch and on the end of each arm was a big leather mitten attached to the canvas sleeves with two straps which when your arms are folded would be buckled together behind your back.

It took me probably 10 or 12 minutes to escape from the jacket, as I had to learn to dislocate my shoulders so that I could undo some of the buckles and get my arms over my head. I did this for approximately a fortnight and felt I had cracked it. Steve organised the challenge with Kathmandu and his team to take place in front of a crowd of people including the Mayor in Cobwebs Nightclub Shanklin. For a time Kathmandu and his team kept phoning me to try and put me off, they were frightened to death that I would achieve this and take the £25,000. They had never seen that type of money before and the fact that I was 100% fit and healthy they knew there was a chance that I was going to show them up on stage and show there was no prize at the end of it.

They had to do something, one afternoon one of his team started ringing me and said there was a problem down at Kathmandu's house and asked if I could give her a hand to fix something that had broken in the office upstairs. So as she and I were quite friendly and she assured me no one else there I said I would join. As I walked into the office Kathmandu and his team all came out of the other rooms and were not going to let me out until I called Steve Harris and called off the challenge. They did leave Leslie, the girl with me in the room that was good of them and although I am sure she knew what was planned, I could see that she didn't like what was happening. I was sure she had quite a lot of feelings for me and had been treated badly by the team. So we spent about an hour there I told her then to go and tell the team that if they didn't let me go immediately I would launch the typewriter through the window into the street and get someone to phone the police and report them for kidnapping. Once she had left the room I rang Steve on his landline and explained what had happened.

Within 10 minutes he was there mob handed and got me out. On the night of the challenge just as it was about to start Kathmandu and his daft team called it off which caused a fight on the stage where the Mayor got knocked off the stage that made the newspapers. I did take off the jacket in 39.4 seconds that would have been a world record but as there were no official timekeepers there in there at the time there was no one there to record it. It really showed them up and put paid to his escapology business. Within a year Kathmandu was killed when cutting a tree down.

My next idea was to get Steve to tow me behind the ski boat on skis and to take off the straightjacket whilst skiing. This took quite a lot of time but finally I conquered it and I wouldn't think there are many people who have done this. Many people watched me that day; whatever made me think of doing that stunt in the first place I really to this day have no idea why?

That summer was quite a hot year. I started dating Sheila Wilson late summer that year; she was a barmaid at the local nightclub in Binstead, which was quite well known and always busy. On a Thursday night it was known as "grab a granny" night, I sure could remember pulling a few.

At the start of September I put my plan into action as regards the poaching. We had three of us on boats and three from the mainland so there were quite a few of us. We needed to be sure that any petrol boats were not monitoring us so we had somebody sat at the marina at East Cowes to keep an eye on the petrol boat that was moored there, also two petrol boats on the mainland were being watched. If they showed any sign of movement we would be informed straight away and we could take action either into Ryde Harbour or Wootton Creek or sometimes we would unclip our oyster dredges and throw them over the side with the oysters that were in 25 kg bags on a long rope. I could usually get everything tied and over the side of the boat in approximately 6 or 7 minutes. Sometimes we would go right up alongside one of the shipping line marker buoys so that when one of the fishery petrol boat went past it would look like just one on their radar. They wouldn't realise we were tied up alongside the marker buoy. It did seem as if I had it all sawn up until the season started on November 1st. However working legally in the daytime didn't seem very interesting at all but it had to be done. The winkles were coming in by the ton as well.

Again we had a fabulous Christmas and New year as always

1987
The second part of the season was going very well as the prices had increased quite a lot. The weather was cold and grey but Sheila and I were having some great times together.

Alan and I were teaching European students to water ski again once the summer came mind you the weather was not always favourable that year. It was quite warm though. On the day of Ryde Regatta we were asked to put on another show of water skiing and para sending, unfortunately as the winds had got up we could not fly the parachute so instead we put on a waterskiing show and taught half a dozen people to ski in front of thousands that were lined up along Ryde seafront. I was a bit concerned as we were leaving it a bit late to get back to our mooring at the top of Wootton Creek, the tide was going out and if we didn't get a move on there would be no water. So, I asked Sheila to join me in the boat from Ryde back to the top of Wootton Creek. I knew I had to take the boat flat out at over 50 miles an hour to get there, so as we set off and rounded the end of Ryde Pier we were faced with 5 or 6 foot waves so we spent most of the next 4 miles flying through the air rather than travelling through water. It took some doing to keep the boat up right and when we got to Fishborne at the entrance to Wootton Creek we had to slow down. I don't have much to say about that experience but it was the first and last time that Sheila would come out on a powerboat with me at least we made it to the mooring just in time. I decided then that I was going to stop teaching at the end of that summer.

That year Stella was pregnant; the baby was due on 21st April 1988, which was my birthday. Sheila was getting quite big quite quickly as well.

In the September we were out on the boats again with the usual lookouts. The fishery officers by this time knew exactly what we were doing. They would come out occasionally to put in an appearance but didn't really bother us very much. About the middle of October Birt Simms and |I put out 3 miles of gillnets for catching fish between Ryde and Bembridge. The following day we went out and we had over 300kg of beautiful cod and about 80ks plaice and 15 kgs bass. What a fabulous haul of fish. We decided to leave the nets down and go back the following day.

The weather forecast that day was saying that the wind was going to strengthen from the south-west through the day and into the night of 16th October, so we went out just after lunch and yes it had become quite strong but we managed to get all the nets back on the boat safely and head back and tie the boat up to the pontoon in Bembridge Harbour. We had a great catch of fish again and were making good money.

As Roger Downer and I ventured out of East Cowes Marina that night to go oyster fishing the wind had started to pick up quite rapidly. We had waves crashing over our trawler and the wind had started to howl. So, getting on for midnight we decided to head back to Cowes Marina and what a journey that was, with the wind and torrential rain, waves, the boat was getting swamped although the water could just run straight off the decks through the scuppers. As we turned towards East Cowes at the lowest point the waves were getting quite mountainous. The only good thing was the fact that there were no other boats on the sea and even all the ferry services to the island had been suspended due to the weather. As we turned around the breakwater and started heading up the River Medina to our moorings the waves were crashing over the front of the boat, we attempted to tie up on our usual birth it was becoming quite difficult as we had already popped two of the fenders on the side of the boat to stop us damaging the pontoon. We then decided to take the boat to a more sheltered part of the marina, it was a good job we did as within half an hour a large catamaran had capsized and got washed down the river and ended up in our mooring. Could not believe how the wind had picked up.

It was well past midnight when we headed home. On the way back there were trees down everywhere and a large furniture van had been blown over on its side in Wootton and debris and all sorts of stuff, fence panels and everything blowing around the roads, it was like a war zone and felt quite unsafe to be out. Roger dropped me off and I went indoors to Sheila. She had been quite worried about us because of the winds. In those days there were no mobile phones to keep in touch. We went off to bed but could hear glass breaking and fence panels and then a tree directly outside our house went over, then the electricity went so we sat up all night listening to the radio. The following morning it was becoming horrendous, as we could see greenhouses smashed all over the road, sheds roof tiles off the houses and trees down, it turned out to be the worst wind we had had on the island, it was a hurricane force. By this time the wind had subsided a bit but looking out we could not go anywhere as every single road was blocked, everyone was out checking the damage to their houses. By the following day we managed to get out and had a drive around on the main roads and saw that Shanklin Pier had been completely washed away with fruit machines and a complete theatre and all sorts of stuff just smashed on the beach.

An oil tanker had gone to ground in Southampton Water and hundreds of boats had been smashed up and sunk on their moorings. Trees were down across the roads, that one night cost thousands of £'s worth of damage but what an experience.

After a couple of days we were back out poaching oysters and also the winkles on the beaches. Because of the hurricane it had swept all the winkles into great big clusters inshore so the pickings were fabulous. It was time to pack up for Christmas and the New Year Break, it was Sheila's birthday as it was the 23rd December and I remember her being quite a big girl due to her being pregnant. We were both really looking forward to our baby being born in 88

I knew that 1988 was going to be a fantastic year for us. The year started off well the shellfish harvest was good that year. I had also started working on the outdoor market; I sold giftware on one stall and fruit and vegetables on the other one.

At the beginning of April Sheila was becoming very big, it was almost as if she were carrying more than one baby. At 3am on the 18th her waters broke and we got ready and took her up to St Mary's hospital. I couldn't stay with her as I had to get back and set up everything on the market stalls and the hospital had said "not to worry it would take ages before the baby is born!" so I wasn't too worried. As there were no mobiles in those days I started running to the phone box and ringing the hospital. Did this twice, on the second time I was told I had a son born at approximately

7.10 weighing 9lbs 13 oz. I had missed the birth so carried on working for the day. I visited Sheila and my newborn son that evening, they stayed in the hospital until the following day when I went to bring them home. I had been working all day in Newport on the market and I felt quite pleased with myself. It was a whole new beginning with a new baby and things were looking great. There was quite a lot of money coming into the house, baby Michael Harry was doing well.

At this time I was driving a brand new Mitsubishi pickup truck that I had bought the previous year but now with the baby I had to get rid of that truck and part exchanged it for a brand new car. I did this and bought an Austin Maestro that was a nice quiet car.

We had a marvellous summer that year, I went water-skiing a few times with Alan and we taught a few students but I was busy as well as I was working the markets 5 days a week and during the summer they were very busy. I took on someone to help me, a chap called Ronnie Hill. We worked well together and he helped on the beaches also picking winkles. I got on with the poaching from September to November and then it was time to go back on the oyster fishing boats. We had a marvellous Christmas that year made better by the fact that we had another smallish person in the house which was so important to me.

1989

At the beginning of 89 we had many orders to fill as regards the Winkles and Oysters. We worked hard that year and coming up to April at home we had all the family with us to celebrate Mike's first birthday. He was growing up so quickly and already into all sorts of mischief.

We started back on the market for the whole summer season. We added another stall selling everything for 50p –it proved to be very busy. We were carrying about 300 different lines. We still had the fruit and veg stall and also the giftware. That summer another thing came onto the market –sand pictures, which you would simply turn over and watch the sand and the oil fall and make beautiful patterns. I actually stood demonstrating the pictures, people were very interested in them.

I had paid £1 each for them, they were delivered straight to my door from Blackpool and I was charging £2.99 each or 2 for £5, sometimes I would sell 150 to 180 a day. I was also selling dancing flowers, as you spoke they would move! Mum and Dad were also running a stall selling gold or silver with English Hallmarks.

In the mornings before going to the markets I would go and do 2 ½ hours picking tomatoes in huge greenhouses in Arreton then carry on to the markets. My friend Ronnie would go and set up the stalls ready for me. The days were long but so worthwhile, Sheila would sometimes come with Mike and he would be watching me work even at that young age.

When we reached September we knew that the petrol boats had decided that it wasn't worth their while as we still had our spies. We had the whole area covered.

However one night we decided to go to Pennington Bay that is the area between Lymington Harbour and Hurst point. We had heard that there were no fisheries boats in the area. There were about 12 boats oystering in the area of Pennington when all of a sudden the whole sky lit up as a police boat had come in between us all and set up a huge parachute flare where the boats were working. Of course they all scarpered, we headed towards the Needles, then back along the coast into the harbour at Yarmouth thinking we were out of the way of it all. Suddenly the same police boat came into the harbour and tied up alongside us. By this time we had taken the oyster dredges off and stored them down below with the bags of oysters that we had caught. The policeman kept saying, "Did you see that flare? I set it off !" He was so excited he was so proud of what he had done. We replied that yes we had seen the bright light and wondered what it was all about. The fast petrol boat had three officers on board and in all the confusion they didn't catch anyone. After this we had fish and chips in Yarmouth, waited for the petrol boat to head back to Cowes we then made our way back to the oyster fishing ground and carried on working. Within half an hour we had a call saying that there was no activity on the fishery officers boats and the police boat had also arrived back in East Cowes, we just carried on working and had a great catch of oysters and a damned good laugh at the police expense. It was a great and profitable couple of months. That year we weighed in 60tons of oysters and 40tons of winkles.

Mike was growing up nicely and was obviously spoilt rotten over Christmas- it was now time to start looking forward to our start on 3rd January 1990. We decided this year to cut our Christmas break, as there had been a great increase in the price of oysters, so we started work again on 27th December. As the second part of the season didn't begin until 4th February we were able to go out poaching instead. On New Years Eve I can remember thinking it would be the quietist night, how wrong we were as we got to our oyster fishing ground at Woodside Bay there were loads of military boats out there training. We couldn't work amongst that lot so we knocked it on the head and headed back to East Cowes Marina and managed to get home just before midnight so that I could see the New Year in with Sheila and our son.

One night we were out and as we came into East Cowes Marina we were apprehended by four fishery officers. They had come over from the mainland. This was because our local fishery officer was away on holiday. As we tied the fishing trawler up they suddenly jumped on us and there was no escape. They then went through 10 bags of oysters weighing 27 kgs each, checking what size they were and found about 25undersized ones. After a couple of hours of Roger Downer and myself winding them up they decided to confiscate 10 bags + a bag of undersized oysters. They had to give us a receipt for said oysters. One particular fishery officer who had a horrible snidey smirk on his face stood on the top of the marina wall and said " never mind lads some you win, some you lose" I then said to him to remember the words he had just spoken. We were nicked and then we made our way home but I knew they were not going to get away with it. I really would have thought that they realized by now that if anyone pisses me off I will get my revenge so, I decided this was going to happen in the next few hours. I got home, had my dinner, had a chat with Sheila and spoke to my dad about it He just said "Don't let the bastards get you down, let's go and get them back"

It was getting quite late, the fishery officers were aboard their boat eating and drinking and having a good laugh at what they had achieved. Their van was parked about 20m from the boat and there was a security chap wondering around the marina, doing his job. However, when he was right up the other end of the marina my dad found something to break the glass whilst I got a marina trolley to put the oysters in. My dad then put the angle line he had found through the back of the hatchback window of the van. This made one hell of a bang but it was quite windy and no-one reacted to it. We waited a few minutes and then took the 10 bags + the small bag of oysters out of the van, pushed the trolley to where our trawler was and put the oysters in bags under the trawler on the seabed. We then brushed all the glass off the trolley and put it back where it belonged.

We then went home. The following morning I was up bright and breezy and I was sat on the Marina wall right next to the van as they surfaced. They could see what had happened to their van and started swearing and going into one about it. When I stood up I said "never mind chaps some you win, some you lose" That made me feel so good I know that they had a lot of explaining to do to the Chief Fishery officer down in Poole.

Of course what they did was report it to the police and they came and arrested me, took me to the police station for questioning, they also got Roger in but he had absolutely no idea about it anyway but of course he suspected it was something to do with me. We went to court and they had their say. Every time the magistrates said anything to them Billy Bowden, the one who sat on the wall that night was told to get the smirk off his face! We found this highly amusing so I stood up and said my piece and so did Roger and made them look like idiots again. I then asked some questions, like as the fisheries had spent so much money trying to find us and catch us and when they finally do they lost all the evidence there was no court case to answer so it was thrown out. As we could have got them from an area that we were allowed to fish in there was no proof of where they came from. The fisheries had to pay back £700 value for the oysters to us + £250 Court costs. On top of that I still had £700 worth of oysters to go and sell.

They were not happy bunnies and every opportunity that they had when we were out working the season they would board us, check our catch and we would just wind them up, saying " You haven't left anything in the back of your van, have you?" We really did give them a hard time and not long after that Billy Bowden was off the scene but was also on the ship to shore radio when the word had got out about what had happened that night. All the other fishermen were messaging us and phoning us and having a great giggle. We knew that the fisheries were listening to the same messages, and the motto of the story is. Don't let the bastards grind you down as they are only educated idiots.

A following night we carried on right through to February. We worked the oysters and winkles until the middle of April and then of course it was time to go back on the market. There were a lot of people over that year the weather was good so money was coming in.

As we did most years the winkle picking gang and myself went to see the Red Arrows and watch the Cowes fireworks. Web ate lots of food and drank loads of beers, it was becoming a bit of a tradition; every Friday after Cowes week Yachting Regatta. At the end of August we would also go and watch the international offshore powerboat racing where the boats raced from Cowes down to Torquay and back at a speed of sometimes up to 100 miles an hour. A lot of these Class one powerboats would be over £1 million, they were over 40 foot long with up to 300hp on two engines, they were usually Lamborghini petrol engines, which made the whole event even better because of the noise of these engines.

By this time Mike was 21/2 years old and into everything. He was very spoilt especially by my dad who took him everywhere.

The winkle picking gangs were back on the beach, I carried on working on the markets until the end of October and at the same time war poaching in the evenings. I must have been working 18 or 19 hours a day. I know Sheila and Ronnie kept the market stall going until 20th December. Overall it had been a good year when we stopped for our Christmas break that year, everyone was healthy and financially we had done very well.

91 dawned very cold, wet and miserable but the work had to continue. Roger and myself decide to fish for oysters in the River Medina which separates East and West Cowes. We could only work 2 hours either side of low water because of other shipping and boats using the river. I loved it down there; there was so much going on, people working on the boats near the riverbanks. It was great, there were so many things that people had dropped off the boats and old bottles that got me thinking again about collecting old Victorian bottles again. We were finding so much stuff, from old watches to old spectacles to outboard engines and handbags. We were also dredging a mixture of different coals that had been dropped by the crane

over many years whilst unloading from the ships hold. At that point I was collecting approximately 100 to 150 kilos a day and over time had amassed over 2 ton of the coal at home. Also the oysters were of good quality so got us a good price and we were the only fishing trawler there.

I managed to get down to Cowes week for the yachting regatta a couple of times and went down on the Friday night to watch the Red Arrows and the fireworks. This as usual was fabulous. On the August Bank holiday it was the Cowes Torquay Cowes powerboat race that was on again. I was down on Cowes Marina early that Sunday to watch the powerboats being lifted into the water and then watched them start the engines, leave the pits and made their way to the start line. The sea was very calm that day, they screamed over the start line at over 100 miles an hour. It was great with a full commentary on how the boats were getting on from all the vantage points en route to Torquay. Suddenly there was a fogbank, they couldn't see anything in front of them and two of these huge powerboats crashed on the beach and got smashed to pieces. The rest of the fleet had to slow down dramatically but once they had turned the mark they were on the way back to Cowes. The winner that year was an Italian in a boat called Iceburg who came screaming over the finish line doing 100 miles an hour.

Back to the markets until the end of September and of course with the poaching of oysters the time went by very quickly and then it was the 8th November and we were off on our very first cruise. We were a bit nervous but when we were welcomed on board we couldn't believe how beautiful it was and we all loved it. It was round the English Channel and the food and entertainment was just perfect. Both Sheila and I knew at that point that that would be the first of many cruises that we would go on.

When we returned home it was a bit of a comedown, we had to get back to the oyster fishing and picking the winkles.

It was time for our Christmas break again. Mike was into everything I remember. At that point I was getting very interested in collecting Old Victorian bottles again. I met up with several people that I had known in the 70's and also some new ones that hadn't been doing it very long

1992. The year started off much the same as usual with the winkle picking and oysters. Money was coming in which was very important to us all. We finished around the middle of April but in the March I decided to start collecting old Victorian bottles again. I managed to contact a few of the old and some of the new bottle collectors one of them being Steve "Shag" Milligan who had a fabulous collection of Isle of Wight bottles. I was mainly interested in the Isle of Wight Stone Ginger Beer bottles so we got together and then started going out digging on the Victorian tips. On one particular evening we decided to head for an area in Cowes called Gubbins and Ball that was a place where the ships would come to the Marina and unload the sand, ballast timber and coal and anything else that had to be transported around the island. On this site there was also where the old steam train used to go past with the railway sidings for picking up goods from the ships. At the time we were not allowed to dig on the Victorian rubbish dump that was next to it but the old bottles were calling out to us so, off we went about 8 pm after dark. We found a lot and about every 2-21/2 hours we would hear the main gates, as the security guards would come to check the site. This was the time we would sit down with coffee and a sandwich and rest. I knew full well that the guards would never come anywhere near us as they stuck to the lights, it was funny as if they were scared of the dark. After about 15 minutes we would hear the gates go again so we could then return to work for another few hours.

One night we were digging on an old part of the tip-it was on a hill. They had built a brand new aluminium building about 80 feet long. After about an hour of digging the whole bank slipped which caused a substantial amount of damage to the building. It was a case of pack up quickly and get out of there.

We made our way from Cowes to Wroxall. We had another site to explore and we found some good bits from Ventnor, which pleased Steve as he lived there. We would do this 3 or 4 nights a week from about 10pm to 5am.

My parents were still market trading and I would be in touch most days to let them know how the bottle digging was going. Dad was particularly interested as he used to collect them in the 70's

After digging through the night times over the course of a few months it was time to try and get permission from the landowner who we believed to be a Mr Rolfe who lived locally as the site of approximately 21/2 acres was starting to look like the top of a pepper pot and the law of averages meant that someone was going to get into trouble for that amount of destruction. It then became imperative that we sought permission with immediate effect. After a while it became clear that I was the one who was going to have to ring him. I thought about it I was quite concerned think I was scared. However I did phone him explaining that some undesirable, people had been digging on his land could we have permission to dig out the site properly. I said my piece and then he said, "Well nipper I don't own the land-it belongs to someone else" I asked then if he could give me the name of the owner. Yes, he said Christine Morton who lives in Upper Ventnor who had recently purchased the land approximately 25 acres from the Isle Of Wight Council. Christine Morton turned out to be a friend of my family. She had a market stall right next to my parents on the market. I was completely gob smacked when I found this out- good job she hadn't asked my parents what Trevor is up at that time.

One night during that summer we decided to go digging in America Wood in Shanklin. I was to meet Steve and another good friend of mine Graham Wheeler there. I was about half an hour late that night and to make a bit of fun I crept through the woods and both of them jumped out of their skins. They had no idea I could come in the other way –this was the first time I had met Graham we have been great friends ever since. That summer we used to go off digging somewhere else, there must have been about 45 of us collecting bottles and other items.

Time continued and one day Dad was talking to Christine, and asked how things were. She said that she was having trouble and explained that she owned 25 acres but people had been going to part of it at nighttime digging for bottles and making an awful mess of it. My dad said it brought back memories of the 70's when he used to go digging for bottles. He said he was too busy to do that nowadays, however he did suggest to her that she go down there at nighttimes and catch them. With this she said she was terrified of going at night as there were lots of holes in the ground and she could really hurt herself and if someone else hurts themselves she was responsible as they were on her land. She said that she was paranoid about holes in the ground even in the daytime. He suggested that she should talk to me and that we could come and have a look. We spent a couple of hours with her talking and put it to her that she could either let people go in and dig until it wasn't worth them digging anymore or let it be done professionally and then completely levelled off so that no-one would want to go there again. It was also a good way for her to earn money from the deal as well.

Well, she then said did I know of anyone who could do this? I replied that I wouldn't mind having a go at this myself considering I had been collecting bottles in the 70's and now we had finished with things like the water skiing etc what I would do is go away and discuss it with her on the Sunday at the market.

On the Sunday I explained to her what the job entailed which was to install a fence around the area with signs up stating that it was private property and anyone caught there would be prosecuted for stealing by finding. We told her that we would have a syndicate of collectors and would pay her £5000 cash for the rental of land for up to a year.

She agreed to this and about this time it was reaching November and of course we were busy back on the Oysters so we couldn't do anything until the New Year. The only problem was that Steve, Graham and myself still had to go up a couple of times a week and make a mess so that she wouldn't know we were responsible for the original damage to the area. One night Graham, Steve, Dougie and myself were just about to leave the site at 4 am we were walking back to our vehicles carrying sacks with the bottles in, shovels and forks. Anyway these two daft policemen walked by us, we all said good morning and we were asked if we were starting work early on the building site to which we said yes we are doing some groundwork before the builders come in at 7am. We couldn't believe our luck, I remember it was quite bad weather and of course we only used to go up there for like quarter of an hour just to make a mess so it looked like someone else had been up there.

I remember the oyster season that year was very successful, we finished on 23rd December and it was decided that Steve and Graham and another good friend of mine Gordon Wilkins and his wife Pat who came from Gosport. They were very keen bottle collectors and used to go up and down the country buying and selling and working all the bottle shows. They had a bottle shop called The Old Bottle Shop in Gosport. The four of us went up there on 23rd December and we had our last dig in –6 degrees we carried on for a few hours and dug up some beautiful pieces that night which was lovely just before Christmas. Over the Christmas my dad called upon another very old friend of mine called Robin Goodridge who was

a very keen collector as well as the rest of us and very knowledgeable. We got together a few times between Christmas and the New Year to decide how we would work it and the best way forward and who we could invite to become syndicate members. We were then ready to announce our plans in the New Year 93. I distinctly 37)remember spending New Years Eve from 6 pm to 5 am seeing in the New Year digging old Victorian Bottles in a field at the top of Wroxall Downs.

Around the end of January 1993 was the date set for the beginning of the dig. We had decided to keep the syndicate to 10 full shares at £1250 per share. There were 8 full shares, one share between two collectors and one share between 3 collectors. This meant a total of 13 syndicate members. My dad was the overall person in charge of the site, Robin Goodridge was manager and Brian was the treasurer. We were working through the first few weeks of January with the shellfish and also still having to make a mess of the site at nighttime. We finally decided to start the dig on February 18th. When we reached a couple of weeks before the start we had a few meetings with the rest of the syndicate and a couple of times on the actual site to explain how we would do the digging. At this point the other members could put forward any suggestions that they had. We then needed to completely fence off the site of 2.1/2 acres with posts and three strands of barbed wire. Steve's dad, Andy Milligan made up a load of signs saying "Private keep out danger." Although he wasn't a member of the syndicate he did help us every day when possible. In fact he and Steve had been collecting bottles for many years.

Christine Morton also had a full share as well as the money we had paid for renting the land. We had one week to go, all the fences were up and we bought an old caravan that we used as an office, we could do our paperwork of our finds and so that we could lock up our tools at night time. We then had a few bushes and small trees to cut down and burn and make the driveway into the site better, as it would soon get muddy with the vehicles in and out.

Finally the 18th arrived and we were all so excited and as we all turned up at the dig at 7am just to have a last chat before we started when the digger turned up at 8 am. As it turned up on the site so did two TV crews and a radio crew and some newspaper reporters. Within minutes of starting the dig we were finding all sorts of good quality items including pot lids, local Ginger Beer bottles and other bits and pieces.

At the top end of the site it was only 7 foot deep but we knew by the time we started to get further down the field it would increase to 45 feet which meant further planning between us to sort out the best way forward. That first day was amazing and it looked like it really was going to be very lucrative. By the end of the first two weeks we were then down about 15 to 18 foot deep and getting deeper each day. By this time we had employed a small Hi Mac to help out as well as the JCB digger. We knew very soon that have to employ a large bulldozer so that the actual bits we were digging we never more that about 12 foot because of cave ins and things happening. The bulldozer was taking 15 to 20mfoot off the top, and spreading it on the left hand side of the tip. As we were stripping it from left to right across the field in 10-foot wide strips we were then going through what the bulldozer had taken off.

Just after 11 am on 2nd March we had a cave in which completely smashed my left leg and after being pulled out and taken back up to the top of the site in a bulldozer bucket I had to be taken home and then up to the hospital to find out what the problem was with my leg. Brian took me home and then my sister took me to St Mary's where they found I had broken my tibia and fibula and needed an operation to screw it all back together. It was a bit of a blow but at least I was still getting my equal share as everything that was dug up was shared equally every two weeks. Anything that we could not share out equally was auctioned off amongst the syndicate members only and that is how we carried on.

After my operation I was in a lot of pain and I remember Sheila and Mike visiting me that night, as I had not been long out of theatre. I had two screws put in my knee I still have them to this day. Mike was only 5 years old at the time and getting quite upset about the fact that I was in hospital poorly. A week later on 8th march they let me out so that I could go straight from the hospital up to the site for the first share out and auction. My Dad and Steve had put all the more common items into crates and boxes and we all had to pick a number and that number would match the items we had in our share. This was organised by the group's treasurer Brian Sheath. It was amazing we all had several hundreds pounds worth of goodies what we could do what we liked with, whether we sold them or swaps and one of the dealers, my friend Gordon Wilkins was up at the site ready to purchase anything that was for sale. Gordon had one third of a share and was buying up as much as possible for his bottle shop in Gosport. In the auction there were some lovely items and I managed to bid and win a Hibberd and co Ginger beer makers small item in the shape of a stone bird feeder which I paid £200 for. This was an amazing item and the first one ever known and within a couple of days I had sold it for £475, everyone went away happy that day, all loaded down with bottles. Gordon and his wife Pat went back to Gosport with a whole van full of all sorts of stuff. So we had made enough money to carry on with the bulldozer and the JCB for the next two weeks. The bulldozer was taking huge amounts of earth off the top of the site and spreading it further across the field so that the digger could dig for it later. We dug strips across the field so that no large cave ins would happen as we kept it to around 12 foot although by now we were approximately 30 foot from the surface but if anything caved in on us it was only 12 foot. I was up there on my crutches and although not doing very much for the first week or two I was able to do bookwork and log all items that we were finding. I had several interviews up there with the TV crew and at least a couple of times a week a newspaper reporter would turn up from all sorts of newspapers.

Jim Baxman was one of the syndicate and very knowledgeable as he had been collecting for many years as was Dave Honeybun another eager collector, an old friend of mine called Nick Jones would come up on site most weekends to have a look around. He is still collecting to this day. One chap I knew called Roy Morgan owned his own magazine that dealt with bottles and other collectable items, unfortunately he was thrown off the site by a unanimous vote along with his girlfriend Andrea Barnes for taking stuff off the site and not paying so his third of one full share was given to Dougie Rigby. The other full share that he owned wasn't renewed which meant that the rest of the syndicate would benefit eventually.

One day a car turned up with a chap in it with a hard hat and a suit so Robin and myself went to investigate who he was and he said he was from the planning department and asked what we were doing. It was pretty obvious with all the crates and boxes of bottles around but I said to him that we were building 2 blocks of flats as we had recently bought the land.

Typical planning department with absolutely no sense of humour said that they knew nothing about this going on and you can't build flats here without planning permission. With this I told him to get a grip and come back down into the real world. We are digging for old bottles as you can see as the last half an hour you have been watching what is going on. He then pointed out to us that it was against planning regulations and that we have to have full planning consent to dig more that 2 mitres under the ground. So, I then annoyed him even more by stating that we are not digging at ground level let alone under it as everything that was put on top of the ground as rubbish. He didn't like being shown up as an idiot but decided that he was not going to win this battle so off he went.

We then decided to cover ourselves by getting the schools involved with our excavation work so we invited Ventnor Middle School and Mayfield Middle School from Binstead up to the site so that they could help out with the excavation and have their own collection of bottles in the schools which proved to be excellent for them and to this day they still own the old bottle collections from that time.

This of course put paid to any daft council staff turning up, as they didn't want to get involved with the schools and their projects.

Every couple of weeks we kept having our shares given to us and the further we went down the field which he did and found it to be absolutely amazing as we were the first lot in the country to use a JCB and bulldozer to dig out a Victorian dump. He managed to take a lot of items back with him much of which we thought was rubbish. He had markets where he could sell it on.

After we had dug approximately half of the site we were taking a couple of days off so that the bulldozer could level off the land that we have already gone through and bring it back to it's former glory. What an amazing time we were having finding some very good items including some amber dumpy cod bottles which were worth £1500 each and these days they are worth even more. By the end of the dig we had found 7 of these bottles.

The weather was good we managed to finish the dig in September after we had followed the bulldozer round as he was levelling off the ground for about a week. We were finding small stuff like pot lid, dolls heads and clay pipes etc and the bigger items like beer bottles and ginger beer bottles. The dig was finally over at the beginning same company Thomas Farrell and were obviously dumped there after he had finished his brewery in 1885. Denis managed to get about 70 of these old ginger beer bottles but the best part was the fact that 7 of these bottles were different to what we had in our collections. We thought there were only 5 variations but it ended up with 12.

The snow was falling all day I remember phoning Graham Wheeler in Bonchurch and because of the snow we decided to meet in Sandown Car Park on the seafront, where we could do some deals on the bottles. Out of my collection I had 7 bottles that were the only ones known and I could have got any price I wanted for them but I wouldn't let them go.

As the weather picked up it was time to go back on the markets although the winkle-picking season was in full swing. I used to work 5 days a week so it was nice to be able to take a couple of days off a week through the summer where we could spend time with Mike on the beach.

At the end of summer we had a couple more places to investigate with the old bottles and this proved to be well worthwhile. The hobby itself was growing from strength to strength especially on the island as we had only the year previous dug the big site at Wroxall. My friend David Orman, would make regular trips to the island from Lymington to join us on our digging experiences.

During this winter I found a 400lb Palliter Bomb that would have been fired from an ironclad warship in about 1880's at Binstead. I rang the police in Ryde and told them. They kept say were we sure it isn't an old drainpipe and stupid things like that. After sometime trying to convince them they eventually said they would send a policeman down to the beach. I told them it was very muddy and to make sure that they had proper Wellington boots on. Ronnie and I waited on the beach for about half an hour and then this young very smart policeman turned up with his normal policeman boots on. I remember saying to Ronnie this is going to be fun especially with him wearing those boots. So we set off across the mud but I did take him on a slightly different route where the mud was really thick and after getting stuck several times and absolutely covered in mud we arrived at the bomb where he started jumping around saying "It's a bomb, it's a bomb!" Well we made our way back up the beach still having to pull him out of the mud, which was so funny as I did tell them to wear proper stuff. A couple of hours later the bomb disposal turned up from Portsmouth but the tide had started to come in so there was nothing they could do until the low tide at 7am. Graham Wheeler had come down the evening just before the tide came in and took some photos of the bomb with us in turn standing on it. So, when the bomb disposal team were asking what it looked like we said we could do better than that we have some photos of it, which Graham had taken down to Boots and had them developed in one hour. They couldn't believe it that we had photos of it within a couple of hours of finding it.

The following morning we helped the police stop people going on the beach whilst the bomb was all wired up. We all had to get behind a wall, which was about 400m away when they shouted 321 and it made an almighty bang and left a 12'x12'x6' deep crater which looked like the surface of the moon. It was all good fun and so back to the winkle picking.

1995 started with heavy snow gale force winds and flooding due to high tides and high winds . There was frost most nights with the temperature down to 7 below zero but we still had to go out onto the beaches to work. Most of January that year was very hard with the wind chill at about −18 degrees By March it was getting a bit warmer so we managed to get a few layers of clothes off.

On April 3rd the brand new ship Oriana Cruise Ship made its way from the shipyard to Southampton. Graham and I went off on one of Marks boats and took some lovely pictures of it. It looked so modern compared to the liners we already had. I could see this was the way of things to come for the cruising trade.

That year Sheila moved in with her sister and brother in law two doors away from us as her brother in law Tom was dying of cancer. He did die on 29th June, which was a very sad day as out of the whole of Sheila's family in my opinion he was normal. The rest of them again in my opinion were alcoholics. Although they were all out at work one of them worked for me for a time but as soon as I gave him wages I would not see him until they all came out of the Star Pub in Ryde High Street. After this happened a couple of times I had to let him go, I didn't have an alternative. At the time Sheila's sister was running a catalogue so every time she needed to place an order she would come round to our house to make a phone call. It reached the stage where every time I came home from work she was on the phone so I said to her why didn't she get her own phone instead of using ours. Her stupid reply to this was why should she when we only lived two doors away. That did it I knew I had to put a stop to it. So, the following morning I went out and bought a coin operated phone, put it on the wall and waited for her to appear. I can remember Graham and I were sat there and Sheila and Mike and as she came in the door she just walked over to the phone and realised she had to put money in it. It was fantastic and really cheesed her off but instead of putting money in our phone box she would rather walk 300 yards down the road to the telephone box

Tom's funeral was on 5th July, which was a sad day. It was hard, having to tell Mike that his Uncle Tom had died, as they had adored each other.

In the August I can remember going out water skiing again. Unfortunately it had been a few years but I did manage to straightaway get up but after 15 minutes I was knackered. That year I took Mike in the swimming over at Abbyfield Bay holiday camp.

On the holiday weekend we watched the race from Cowes but this year there was an awful tragedy as one of the Abu Dhabi teams boat which was a wide catamaran 40m foot in length and 15 foot wide flipped over at over 100 miles an hour just off Ryde, killing one of the crew. This was very sad and the team who had 3 boats in the race decided not to race for the weekend. I was watching the petrol boats that year whilst the others were out poaching for oysters until the start of the season. Winkles were fetching £25 per 25kilos and oysters £2 per kilo. This year I worked with Pete Holbrook and his son for the official Oyster season and there were so many out there. During the evening I would go with Roger Downer to the River Medina and we completely cleared that river of oysters. None of the other fisherman knew we were there because we had been working all day but we had the stamina then. Mind you I can honestly say that between winkles oysters and the markets we desperately needed the Christmas break. It had been a long year and the weather had turned again to frosty and cold.

Out of all the years in the 90's I think this one was one of the worst I remember. Bitter cold winds, snow, freezing rain that made working on the beaches very difficult as we were carrying heavy loads of shellfish off the beach. The month of January seem to drag so did February so when the decent weather arrived it was nice and pleasant.

That spring we did a dig in Shanklin and found some amazing stuff which really boosted our collections. We also made money selling to our dealers, Gordon Wilkins and Dave Orman. That dig was one of the best three weeks we have ever done.

Back on the markets in the summer this time selling baby ware and giftware which proved to be very profitable but we were only doing it three days a week so that we could get on with other things we wanted to do. One of those things was to make one mile of fishing nets, which would have a float line on the surface and lead line on the bottom. We could use it in 6 to 8 foot of water; it would bag out underneath the water and catch anything that went near it. It took approximately three weeks for Ronnie and I to make and sew all the net together. Once we had put it in the water from our small boat we were catching so many fish and the boat was only a 14-foot rowing boat and we were working in shallow waters. We were catching hundreds of kilos of grey mullet which was sold to the Indian market traders three days a week also lots of sea bass which went to the hotels. As we were getting a fabulous price for this we carried on through the Autumn when we were back poaching again.

Pete Holbrook and myself went to Southampton to view a fishing trawler that was for sale. Pete decided to buy it but we had to do work on it to bring it up to the standard that we wanted it to be. It was a fabulous boat, a Versatility 30 foot. There were other boats out with us and of course as with other years we had people watching the petrol boats.

The year was financially fabulous and was running well but I wanted more, so, I teamed up with Dave Long and we started doing warehouse parties with clothing and underwear et cetera. We would take the stuff to peoples houses and they would do a warehouse party for us of course this got around and we were able to do so many it became an amazing business. I was able to go out on the boat and on the beaches.

This was the year that Sheila passed her driving test which made things a lot easier for picking up stock for the market stalls and also for shopping and taking and collecting Mike from school.

On 12th December Sheila and a crowd of us went on the QE 2 for a trip, which was lovely just before Christmas, which was just what we needed. When we returned I worked the oyster season with Pete

Holbrook. The price of the oysters was £2000 per ton. Later in the evenings Roger Downer and I would go straight back out on his boat and work the river to get a few bags of good quality oysters that we had a special market for.

Now was the time for our Christmas 10 daybreak, which was needed, it had been an amazing year as always, everything running smoothly and everyone relatively fit and healthy. Of course it went by so quickly and we were straight back to work at the beginning of 1997

This year we had an awful lot of people visiting the island so of course the markets were very busy. We still did giftware, baby ware and more fruit and vegetables. The fact that Sheila had passed her test helped a great deal with deliveries and I was very grateful to her. It made things run much more smoothly with her help.

That year Sheila, Mike and myself went on a fabulous cruise on the maiden voyage on the brand new Cruise ship called The Vision of the Seas.

My dad on the other hand was getting huge rewards for selling his gold and silver plus diamond rings. This meant that money was rolling in by the thousands and of course he needed it at the time as he was building a new bungalow and paying with cash to fund it. There was also huge amounts of fake clothing and shoes and perfumes that were flooding the market. I got involved with this, I knew they were fake but to be honest they were of better quality than the real ones. There was also thousands and thousands of litres of booze going around for sale which I could make money on. A lot of local shops were selling this booze from behind the counter as were the cheap cigarettes that had been imported. Even the police were in on this as one of my friends was supplying them. They obviously used it towards Christmas for their friends and family the same as what we did.

However, I remember it getting out of hand and that was the cue for me to walk away and start back on the shellfish and out on the oyster boats poaching right through September to December. We worked that year in Langston Harbour as we had heard there was a lot there as we had been into Osborne Bay for so many nights.

1996

Once again the weather started off badly and this year I decided I didn't want to work as hard as I had been doing over the previous years. Wanted to concentrate on digging for bottles and selling a lot of my collection. That year Lenny Hodges and I went digging down at an old pig farm just outside Ryde . It turned out to be very successful even though we were not using a machine. It boosted our collections.

However, we were on the lookout for new sites to dig. We knew we were going back to Wroxall to have a dig up there. So, Steve Milligan, Lenny Hodges and I went up there in July with a machine. It was a JCB digger, which was brand new. Unfortunately the driver reversed it straight into a 20-foot hole and all you could see was the front and the bucket. The driver was okay but had to ring his boss who in turn came out to see what had happened. He then called for a huge crane to come and lift the digger out but because the ground was so soft as we had already dug into it. The small of the two cranes would lift the JCB out but in case the crane started to sink as we had already dug this area. The larger crane was purely there to winch the smaller crane out should it have when boss turned up he was more interested in what we had dug up rather than his digger

Once it was lifted out we resumed digging again.

At this time a cargo ship carrying fruit called Doll America that had crashed into the nab tower and had a lot of damage to it. It was beached at Bembridge on the mud banks as she was taking on a lot of water and had to have a survey done before it could carry on. For a couple of weeks we were finding all sorts of fruit on the beaches, wooden crates of pineapples, oranges and apples. It was lovely, just needed washing off, it was fine. There were also lots of bottles of spirits and big pouches of tobacco and cigarettes that were in waterproof packaging so that was also fine. We made good money on it all.

In the spring we bought a burger van and we were able to cook all sorts including jacket potatoes. We were outside Bobby G's Disco beside Waltzing Waters for quite a time and this proved quite lucrative.

During that summer I became a shareholder at Isle of Wight speedway and also assistant starter at the starting gate every Tuesday evening. I also owned the track shop nearby which supplied all sorts of clothing etc.

August bank holiday weekend for four days we had the sole catering rights to feed 6500 scooter riders who were there for the weekend. We worked 24 hours a day for four days and took thousands of pounds. The burger van certainly served us well that year.

The following day we were back digging with the JCB again and taking a lot of stuff out of the ground. It was then time to start back on the winkles and the poaching at the end of September until 1st November when the oyster season started.

I had a lot of plans for the New Millennium and after a wonderful Christmas we went on Woodside Bay Beach at midnight on New Years Eve listening to the ships foghorns and the thousands of fireworks that were set off all along the south coast.

On the 3rd January it was all systems go and the first time out to work in the new century

Welcome to the year 2000

Again we started with very bad weather. The only good thing about the weather being bad was the fact that the shellfish was fetching wonderful prices.

Getting into March I kept feeling overtired which was quite unusual for me as I didn't sleep much as I would be out working most of the day and night. By April I was starting to feel quite poorly at times and really didn't know what the problem was. It was my 40th birthday on 21st April and on that day Sheila, Mike Myself and 13 of my friends from York came down and we spent 5 days at the Grand Hotel Sandown. John Williams was one of them with his wife Dorothy. They had brought the powerboat down 2 jet skis and all the skiing equipment so we all looked forward to a fabulous time. After this seven of us went to the British Grand Prix at Silverstone in a beautiful white limousine that made us feel very special. We had a wonderful time but still I had that horrible niggley feeling of being poorly.

The following day we were all down at Woodside Bay by the beach with the powerboat and the jet skis and doing lots of skiing and all the other waterborne activities. It was making me feel so tired though. At the time I was still working the markets three days a week. I remember picking Ronnie Hill up who had been helping me for so many years on the markets. I would be stood at the back of the lorry unloading the stock and quite often he would come back for the next load I would be already asleep on the floor in the back of the lorry. Later that day another market trader also called Trevor said that he reckoned that I might have Diabetes like he had. I was feeling very faint and was asleep under the stall where no one could see me. Trevor came and found me and tested my blood. With that he gasped and said "Bloody hell you should be dead you need to go to the hospital" As it was only an hour to go until the end of the market we got packed up as soon as we could. Ronnie drove the van home whilst Sheila took me straight to the doctors in Ryde. He checked my blood again and sugar levels and everything else and confirmed that I was definitely diabetic. My sugar was at a dangerously high level and I could quite easily go into a coma. The doctor decided that I should be taken straight away to St Mary's in Newport. When I got there I was put straight onto a drip, had all sorts of injections and stuff put in and stuff taken out, I felt so weak, couldn't argue.

That was pretty much it for me work wise. Ronnie and Sheila kept everything running with the markets through the summer, as I knew they would. This took a lot of worry away from me whilst I was recuperating.

The summer of 2000 was very hot and we had an enormous forest fire in Park Hurst Forest near to the prisons and another massive fire in Firestone

Copse Wootton. This was very hard for everyone concerned particularly the fire service.

I could not take part in any oystering or gathering of shellfish as I was too poorly and totally laid up. At the time I was sleeping for around 18 hours a day as it took months to get my sugar levels back to normal. During October and November there were huge floods and storm force winds which caused a lot of problems on the island with landslides, homes flooded and all sorts of trees down and it just would not stop raining.

As I was still quite ill I had plenty of time to think about the future and what to do work wise I knew I still wanted to work on the beaches.

Christmas came round, lots of visitors came to see how I was, everyone was concerned about me but we had a great Christmas and New Year went very well.

2001

For the first few months of this year I was still feeling pretty rough and had no motivation to do a lot but I knew I had to do something or I would lose everything I had.

This carried on for some time but in June we all went on holiday to St Lucia in the Caribbean for two weeks, which was absolutely beautiful. There were quite a crowd of us and the weather was so hot out there -a wonderful holiday. Our 13 friends came back to the island so that we could have another week of water skiing over here and went out for some lovely meals until it was time for me to go back on the beaches and clam fishing.

This year of course was the year that New York was attacked by two aircraft that finally brought the twin towers to the ground and killing thousands of people. It was the biggest terrorist attack that the world had ever known.

I remembered back in the early 70's when we were putting large clams that we couldn't sell back into the river at Newtown Creek and I started to think had they reproduced? After a few weeks trying to get motivated I decided to take a trip down to see what the situation was. Brian Newton and I went and after about an hour wondering along the creek we spotted a few dead clamshells. They were quite small in size but we knew then that they must have reproduced. We made our way into the river and started digging with our bare hands and found tons of perfect size clams. We knew we were on to a winner.

We also knew that was owned by the National Trust. They had bought the whole area and creek from Swainston Manor in 1965 with all the fishing rights. When you have fishing rights the species of fish or shellfish have to be named in any paperwork. I knew instinctively after I had done my homework on it that we were free to roam anywhere on the land and also the fact that we had introduced the clams there in the early 70's Unfortunately the National Trust didn't see it that way at all and were out to cause trouble because they thought they were right and felt superior to the rest of us.

After a few months we were taking many tons of clams away. We were working twice a day for 21/2 hours per tide. At the same time I teamed up with a chap called Dave Fogden from Emsworth who was running Wootton fisheries for a company called Portsmouth Seafoods. He spoke to the boss of this company called Albert who was probably the best and largest buyer of clams from all over the world. We knew we had a great market for them. So, with Brian and Dave we took on Paul and David Lambert to work for us and the five of us were absolutely earning a fortune right under the noses of the National Trust. They were giving us a lot of trouble, threatening all sorts of things, yet all the time I knew there was nothing they could do as they had as much right to the clams as we had. I also knew I had prescriptive rights since the 70's I was however not going to tell them this as I knew it was really winding them up and getting to them. They then went down to try and find our body boards that we used so that we didn't sink in the mud and our fish baskets that we used to hide. A couple of times they did manage to find them and stole them and also our little boat that we were using to cross to the other side of the river.

One night as we came out of the creek and walked the mile through the woods to the road where we had parked, another white van was there and as we approached this driver got out and informed us that he was a National Trust warden and was going to confiscate our catch. As far as I was concerned I thought he was a complete idiot when he said that the clams had been there since Roman times and that they are private and that we are not allowed to take them. His name was Davey. So he took our clams that night and first thing in the morning when the tide was in Brian and I went down to Newtown to watch what Davey was doing. He came up the river in the National Trust boat and tipped our clams over the side of the boat where we had got them from. That evening we were back to pick them up thinking at the time anyone with half a brain would have put them in deep water so that we couldn't get them.

Soon after this there was a meeting at Shalfleet Village Hall regarding the National Trusts plans for the Newtown creek area. So Brian and Paul Lambert, Dave Fogden and I attended and when they had finished their little speech telling us all what they were going to do it was my turn to say my piece, I had everyone clapping and cheering me on for putting the National Trust down. Shortly after this I was approached by Andrew Turner who was the local MP for the island. He believed that I had prescriptive rights, as did other government bodies. I had a few meetings with our MP and he took it to the House of Commons regarding what happened on the 4th September, when, as we got out of the river there were 9 police officers hiding in the woods and they surrounded us as we reached the road. The road had been closed at both ends, which was absolutely diabolical even ridiculous as all we were doing was taking clams out of the mud that we had put there. So nine police officers to fishery Inspectorates to National Trust wardens and a harbourmaster were just banging their lips together as if they knew what they were talking about but obviously didn't. They were about to confiscate our catch of about 210 kg of clams but I was not going to let them have them without a proper written receipt. The police thought that we were dirty tramps picking clams and had to take the National Trusts side. Little did any of them know we were earning in three hours what they earned in a week. They were very short sighted but all they saw was that we were in the wrong.

After a good row with them there was no way they were going to take them as far as I was concerned. Then unbelievably, the best thing happened. The representative of the National Trust did not have anything to write on to give me the receipt so the police wrote a receipt on Hampshire Constabulary paper. This caused quite a stir when the following day I reported it to the MP who immediately took it back to Parliament and the police got a rocket for it. I have the letters here with me that I shall publish with the book. I also have all the newspaper cuttings as well. I was absolutely loving it, knowing that these idiots had absolutely no idea what was going on they couldn't see that we were taking thousand of pounds per year of clams from the creek. I offered to pay them £1000 per year as a goodwill gesture but Tony Tutton and Robin Lang who were in charge didn't want to know they were so convinced that they were in the right so we carried on fishing until Christmas. Still solicitor's letters were coming from the National Trust and the MP and the House of Commons moaning about the police and their activities and also letting the National Trust dig themselves a very deep hole. In fact the more I laughed at them the more they were getting wound up. It was becoming such a big issue on TV and radio and newspapers that people were coming down to Newtown at the low tide just to watch us and see what we were doing. We had people leaving letters on our vehicles saying that the National Trust had been looking in our vehicles with the doors open. The National Trust kept on stealing our body board and baskets again and just kept on about something they had no idea about.

Through the latter part of 2001 we were getting tons of crabs, lobsters and oysters as well as many tons of clams.

I remember one day Dave Fogden turned to me and said he didn't know how I could tackle the National Trust and show them up to be such idiots adding that I must have balls big enough for a dump truck! At the end of the year Dave decided he would be leaving Wootton Fisheries and going back to Emsworth to spend more time with his wife and carry on working on the beaches over there so, I was in charge and running the business and also getting a good wage packet each week on top of what I was getting from elsewhere. What an incredible year I had had I couldn't wait to get back to my battles with the National Trust in the New Year

This year 2002 we were still at war with the National Trust. They had sold the fishing rights to Peter Blackman of Puffin Fisheries in 1989 and he sold them back to the National Trust in 1996 or thereabouts. Neither had any right to do this, they had sold it to him for many thousands of pounds. The National Trust then decided that they would put the clan fishery up for tender. They put an advert in the local press and one of the local shellfish dealers John Chandler from Southampton decided that it was a good thing and he could make thousands of pounds from it so, he paid his money but never got anything from it as they didn't own it to sell to him. This carried on for several weeks, we were down there days taking the clams out from under their noses.

The police turned up again and threatened us with arrest if we didn't come out of the water and talk to them. One was really an ignorant arsehole, he thought he was so hard all he said to me was "Oi get out of that river now I want to talk to you" I simply turned around and in my quiet voice and said "Sorry are you talking to me and if so it doesn't cost anything to be polite" He was jumping up and down, waving his arms around he said again to get out of the river now pleassse! I then turned to him and said no I was working. He really did blow a gasket then screaming and shouting and the other two coppers were just stood in the background. We just carried on until the tide came in but rather than take the clams out and have them confiscated we simply tied the sacks up and left them on the riverbed. Then we came out covered in mud we were marched about a mile through the woods where the ground was so uneven we accidently bumped into the three policeman with beautiful white shirts on and unfortunately they did get a bit muddy. These things do happen and when we reached their vehicle we all had to stand in a line. We were tired so we leant on their van that of course showed 5 outlines of men covered in mud on their crisp white van… It was time then to really wind them up. So the gobby one then decided that we were all under arrest but having discussed it with his colleagues decided that they would not arrest us as the back of the van would have been full of mud and they would have had to clean it. However this sort harassment carried on daily. We in the meantime just carried on working.

The TV crews and radio reporters had been down for a chat and had filmed us on several occasions. After a while the National Trust realised that they had no rights to the clams but the harbour officers and the fishery offices were not having any of it. What the hell it had to do with the Southern Sea fisheries God only knows as it is outside of their area.

So many people were backing us, they would visit us just to have a chat as they didn't like the way the National Trust does things.

The National Trust owed me a substantial amount of money as they had stolen equipment from me and my workforce. They had taken bags of clams and never returned them and they had also called me a thief over which I intended to take them to court. How those idiots ever got the job I cannot imagine but I am sure that when Tony Tutton had to sign a cheque he must have been seething with anger. As for the police they really are the dumbest people around especially here on the island. I must say it is always good to be one step ahead of them it is great fun keeping them behind you.

All through the 90's and up to about 2005 at home we had a police scanner, which was crystal clear and could hear everything that was going on with the police on the island. Quite often I would hear my name come up on it that was quite amusing. At the time Sheila and myself were working on the markets.

When we arrived home that day it turned out that Mike, because of an argument with the teacher had left the school and come home. He went straight upstairs and put the scanner on. He then heard that he was missing from school and sure enough the police turned up at the house. He didn't answer the door and eventually they went away.

When we returned from work he told us what had happened, then we had the school on the phone being pathetic. After this the police turned up again and I dismissed them telling them I couldn't be bothered to listen as I had to get to work on the beach.

We use to have that scanner on 24 seven for 15 years and it was only when they went digital that we couldn't pick anything up. At nighttime I would sometimes be woken up be it a car chase or burglaries going on. It was weird listening into Ambulance, Fire, Coast Guards, mobile phones and any aircraft that were flying around including the big airlines

In 2003 we were battling strong winds and very cold weather making it very difficult to get the clams out. The National Trust were still giving us grief, people were telling us that their representatives were still looking in the back of our vans. However, they then called a meeting at the Council offices and we all agreed to it. There was supposed to be several of the top people from the National Trust attending and that said Mickey Cox, Brian Newton and myself went to the offices where we were shown into a room where there was food and drink. Shortly afterwards we got the message that there was a delay and the five members of the National Trust would be late arriving so, we ate all the food and drank all the coffee and then left them a note apologising for the fact that we couldn't wait around as the tide was going out and we needed to be down at the Creek to fish for the clams. I really do not know how much the food and coffee had cost them plus the travelling from the mainland as there were some of the top people from the National Trust. On one point I am sure and that is that they must have been spitting feathers. The reason I did this was not only to wind them up but to see how they would react of which there was no reaction at all so then I knew that I was correct in my thoughts that they knew that they didn't have any legal rights at all.

From that I spoke to Tony Tutton and Robin Lang and told them straight that if they didn't leave me and my workers alone, giving us permission to drive down through the woods and onto the quay and also give us a key to their gate and allow us to put a small boat of about 12 feet with a small engine onto the quay as and when we needed it. If this wasn't adhered to and there were any problems whatsoever I would make it common knowledge that Newtown Creek is a public fishery for anyone who wants to go there and pick clams and other shellfish.

Well, this hit the National Trust hard as they knew they had lost this ongoing battle so they decided that we could have a months trial but I decided that I also wanted a fishing trawler there to dredge for clams and oysters. They had to agree.

A couple of days later a very good fisherman Kipper Marshall from Southampton turned up with his dad Colin in a 30 foot trawler called the Benjamin Guy. They couldn't believe how I had swung this in our favour, as this was July and the oyster season finished in March, no one could do anything about it as it was outside of the southern fisheries area. After the boat had been re-rigged Kipper and Colin would steam over from Southampton every morning, meet with Mike my son. They would then go back down the river and catch 10 bags of oysters weighing about 27 kgs each and then Mike would bring them back on the little boat and unload them into his van. Kipper and Colin would then steam back to Southampton. We carried on doing this five or six days a week for a month and then took another two weeks that we decided we were going to have. Mike or sometimes myself would bring the oysters back as quite often I I found out that the National Trust Harbourmaster had been each morning going round all the Yachts and pleasure craft in Newtown Creek and taking money from them for their overnight stay. I wanted to check if this was legal which I found out it wasn't. As Newtown Creek was known as an arm of the sea the harbourmaster could only go round with a bucket and ask for donations. By my finding this out it really upset the National Trust. They had been doing this for many years and had got away with it. As they had been making things difficult for me I intended bring them down a peg or two.

On another occasion there was a bloke on a boat and he pretended that he had a gun and was shooting at us on the trawler that we were working on. He seemed as if he was a complete idiot so we reported him to the police. Later we found out that he was the local gentry as he called himself the Lord of the Manor. We insisted that the police go and visit him or we would take the law into our own hands. So off they went and really wrapped his knuckles Lord of the Manor or not, just an educated idiot as far as we were concerned, a silver spoon stuck up his backside from what he had been left by his parents.

We cleared all the oysters making thousands of pounds in those 6 weeks but we had more plans. It was time to get our friend, Paul Lambert, one of our team to bring his trawler in and start digging up the place for clams. We would be there hand picking where the trawler couldn't go. The rest of the year was going well we were taking in so many tons of crabs and Lobster at our unit and many tons of winkles also coming through but we were concentrating on the clams as we knew they would be there for many years to come. We moved them around so that they would come on to the size we needed. We also knew exactly where they were.

Around October there was an incident where we had a phone call from the police saying that Mike and his friend Matt Honeybun had to be taken down to the police station straight away for making racist remarks at school. The kid involved had very slightly darker skin and kept calling Mike "Ginger top" and because of this they were calling him "Gary". I should explain to anyone reading this there is one episode of "Only Fools and Horses" where a boy in his late teens with slightly dark skin ended up in Dell and Rodney's flat, having been found in the back of Denzel's lorry between pallets of crates of beer when he returned from France. Well this character was called Gary, so when this kid started calling Mike and Mat names they replied in a Pakistani accent "Gary!" Subsequently the boy went home and told his father who rang the police. I am afraid when I took the call I just laughed I thought it was someone geeing me up. However, what made it worse was the fact that the copper on the phone was called PC Witt and I found this highly amusing.

I took Mike down as requested and Denis Firth took Matt Honeybun as well. When we arrived

Mike was arrested and I then asked to ring my solicitor Mr Ronald Gold. Having told him what had happened he laughed and said he would be there in an hour. Mike and I were put into a room with a phone. I had said I needed to call Mike's mum to let her know what was happening so the silly sod gave me a number to get a clear line out of the police station. I didn't need to phone Sheila, as she was quite aware of what was going on as she was in the house when the phone call came through! I then proceeded to ring my uncle Norman in Canada and was on the phone for about 45 minutes until the solicitor arrived.

We were all then taken to a room, tapes were switched on to record everything as Mike was being questioned. Of course the solicitor and myself started laughing and so did Mike at that point. The copper didn't find it funny to which I replied, "I thought you would with a name like yours!" Both the solicitor and myself couldn't contain ourselves we were crying with laughter with tears running down our faces. Mr Gold said he had never heard anything so bloody stupid in all his life and soon after this we were told we could go. Denis went in next with Matt and much the same thing happened. The copper still didn't find it amusing. Matt was told he could go as well. I am not sure what happened after this but I think I can remember the other kid had some sort of accident-bless him!

That year was particularly busy. We had shipped over 100 tons of shellfish from out unit factory over to the mainland to be exported to France and Spain. Winter 2003 was very cold very quickly and by the end of the year it was a pleasure to have our 10 days off just to recharge our batteries and think how we were going to tackle the National Trust in the New Year would be on the boat; they were then taken to our unit in Wootton and sorted out before being taking over to Portsmouth Seafoods on the mainland. The harbourmaster proved to be a bit difficult but we threatened him with the fact that we could contact the trawlers immediately, which stopped him.

2004
After a horrible start to the year where the weather made work very difficult. Travelling was also very

bad; we had cut our clam fishing down to one week a month on the biggest tides, as the water was so cold. For the rest of the months between January and April we concentrated on picking up Winkles and oysters from the beach. We did have a few run-ins with the National Trust but simply told them to go away so it wasn't too bad.

With the amount of money we had been earning we decided to buy a mobile home at Woodside Beach Holiday Park in Wootton, although still sticking with the oysters, clams and winkles. We advertised our mobile home and straight away we were fully booked until the end of 2004. Sheila and I couldn't believe it, at the time we wished we could have more homes to rent out. It was a beautiful site right on the beach and in the height of the summer July and august we were charging £520 per week for it. At the end of June we purchased another one, which again we managed to fill up for the rest of the summer and into the autumn. We then registered the business known as Red Squirrel Holidays Ltd. This renting business was going from strength to strength we had advertised in a couple of Internet sites and by the Xmas we were fully booked for the following year 2005. In the September we bought our third mobile home and when one of them was free for a few days Sheila and myself + our little puppy would go down there. She was a lovely little border collie, Doris.

As we got to the end of the summer even though we were working on the shellfish we knew that Mobile home number four would have to be purchased as soon as one became available. Eventually, a mobile home that was owned by some friends of ours, Tess and Pete was up for sale so we bought it just before Christmas and once again it started filling up for the following year.

We were doing so well I didn't go back on the trawlers; I concentrated on buying all the shellfish, picking on the beach and working on the rental business.

We put in a lot of effort and it turned out to be an amazing year. As the October came which was the end of the season I decided to put brand new decking areas for the mobile homes to make them look so much better. I used a natural timber as the site was in a wooded area. Sheila and I used to go down there about three times a week just to do all the jobs, decorate, put new carpets in and get them ready for the opening on 1st March 2005.

Unfortunately the managers of the site were absolutely useless, nobody liked them, they were awful, they were ripping off the company who owned the site but I gave them a warning not to interfere with what I was doing otherwise I would make their lives a misery. So, they took that on board and we were able to respect each other, but my plan was more long term. I wanted them and their dozy son who pretended he was a gas fitter off the site. I could see that there was something very dodgy going on so I had to bide my time I would get them off the site. I did however; speak to Rotch Property Group Management Company called Prime Estates. His name was Peter Bohm and he proved to be invaluable over the next few years in getting my plan off the ground.

Through December we had a massive surge on the clams and the price went right up and we made an absolute fortune in that month. The usual Christmas celebrations were wonderful as they always were but we knew that we would be facing the elements in 2005

2005 started the year a lot warmer thus making working conditions much easier in the water. We were able to get our first haul of clams in and also a good catch of winkles and oysters as prices are usually better in January than at any other time of the year. The weather however did deteriorate somewhat through February but the shellfish kept coming in and we were also getting ready to open at the caravan in March.

We knew however that the managers would be their usual horrible selves and would not help anyone and pretty much made life awkward for the owners. The first couple of weeks we had two of our caravans booked so we took advantage of the fact that we could stay in the other one for a week that meant that we could have a holiday and relax. This we were only able to do on the odd weekend throughout the summer as well.

In April we met Bill and Julie Chittil, they were from Waterlooville who were down most weekends. We had some magic times together as Bill used to go on the beach gathering shellfish to cook at his mobile home

In the June Stella and I went on a four night cruise on the QE2 which meant one day at sea, a trip to Cherbourg in France then the day back across the channel to the Solent where the QE2 had been chosen to be the flagship to the fleet at Spithead. This was to celebrate the 200th anniversary of the Battle of Trafalgar. In the Solent that day were hundreds of warships from all over the world, tall ships, cruise ships, tankers, cargo ships, fishing trawlers and tugboats and thousands of pleasure craft all waiting to see the Queen and her family come past to review the fleet.

On the morning of the 28th June instead of being at the heart of the celebrations we were anchored off Seaview instead of Spithead that was three miles away. I was disgusted at this and teamed up with a chap called Ian and his wife Mavis. The four of us decided that we would tackle the captain about our anchoring position. They had put a chart on the library wall and there was no way that we could clearly see anything of the celebrations from where we were. So, armed with the brochure, given by the travel agent we arranged to meet the captain who straightaway decided to treat us like idiots and informed us that the water wasn't deep enough at Spithead so we had had to anchor where we were for safety reasons. I asked him how come we had sailed from Southampton to where you should have anchored off today, don't try to pull the wool over my eyes as I have been a trawlerman for over 30 years in the Solent and know everything there is to know about the tides and certainly how deep it is. He tried to palm us off with other rubbish and I ended up telling him he should not be in charge of a cruise ship perhaps he should go and be the master on a tug boat which he was not happy about. He then left the ship and went to one of Navy Aircraft Carriers HMS Illustrious.

Meanwhile, the four of us started a petition outside the library on board the ship. I telephoned the BBC and ITV, Radio Solent, Isle of Wight radio and

Isle of Wight TV and also several newspapers. My son Mike and his then girlfriend Amy Jones were on Ryde seafront watching the celebrations and as I had been talking to him from the ship he knew exactly what was going on, should he be interviewed by the TV which he was. I had a live video interview from the ship, which was put out over the tannoy along the island coast and Portsmouth and Southsea. There were thousands of people on the seafront.

My phone never stopped ringing that day. Friends and family were listening to the video. The TV companies and radio stations were wanting interviews, it was quite a big story but it wasn't until later that day that we found out that the reason this had happened and we were anchored 3 miles away was because Canard were given their anchor ring position six weeks prior to the event but forgot to confirm it. Of course we were stuck where we were, there was nothing we could do. The captain never came back so another one was sent, Master Bates, which caused everyone to have a giggle.

The following day as we arrived back in Southampton there were loads of TV cameras there, radio reporters, newspaper reporters and photographers. We were stuck in that cruise terminal for 3 hours and when we arrived home we contacted a solicitor in Birmingham and managed to get it on a no-win no fee basis and everyone got their money back plus 35% compensation. Canard Line are a great company and the QE2 is a wonderful ship but when these big companies mess up they have to pay the penalty.

The rest of the summer was fabulous and in the October we had two interviews for the programme Holidays from Hell with Trevor MacDonald, which was filmed on Ryde Seafront and some at my parents home and our caravan park at Woodside Bay.

We were very busy the rest of the time renting the caravans out and still on the clams oysters and winkles. The caravan park closed on 31st October then it was back to the shellfish to hit it hard for a couple of months until our Christmas break

2006

In January 06 Michael passed his driving test which took half the workload off me regarding driving and delivering the shellfish. Quite a lot of cold snowy weather was still around for January and February so we only stuck to one week a month on the clams and the rest of the time on the winkles and oysters.

In the April we had another meeting with the National Trust as they wanted to know other things but I made it clear to them that it was none of their business and anything we were doing really didn't have anything to do with them. They kept getting quite uptight they really had to watch their step otherwise I would have sued them for all the stupid things that they have done.

In May we purchased another caravan for the site and were getting on with all the bookings that we were getting. It was amazing the mobile homes looked beautiful inside and out with all the new decking and freshly painted inside. Every time a guest turned up they would receive a gift pack, which consisted of a bottle of red wine and one of white from the local vineyard on the island with our own labels on. There was also a pen and pencil telephone book notepad and ruler with Red Squirrel Holidays Ltd written on all the items. We also gave them some postcards to send to friends of the actual mobile home they were staying in thus we got more bookings for the site. This year I decided that any bookings that I had to pass on to people on the site I would take 20% from and as they were filling up their mobile homes everyone was happy. They were making lots of money.

The summer was great we were also taking lots of clams and oysters from Newtown Creek as we had Paul Lambert still with us with his trawler. On the 4th September we were back onto the poaching of oysters in Osborne Bay on average taking about half a ton per night. One afternoon we locked ourselves into in our unit where there were huge holding tanks for shellfish. There was a hammering on the metal door; it was Graham the fisheries officer. He thought that Paul and Mike were the only ones in there. We would not let him in he kept saying that I had let him in and that he had his rights to search the place. Obviously, we couldn't let him in as we had over two tons of poached oysters that were in one of the tanks. We were sorting through a load of oysters and loading them into our van, as these have to be taken to the mainland. We carried on working and he carried on getting soaking wet in the rain outside him still knocking on the door hoping to come in.

At this point I went into my office and rang Albert who was the boss of Portsmouth Seafood's and explained to him that there would be a delay due to the idiot that was banging on the door. After about an hour and a half he was getting quite stroppy, as he was cold and wet, I went to the doors and hammered on them with 2 hammers. With this he dropped all his paperwork and clipboard and mobile phone. He didn't know that I was in there until I unlocked the door and as I did Mike flew out with a van full of oysters on his way to the mainland. So, I asked the fishery officer what he wanted and he said that he understood that I had been getting oysters and that he was coming to search the place. My reply was he was not getting in until I saw some sort of identification. He then said, "Don't be so bloody stupid Trevor you know who I am!" and again I said not until you show me some ID. He then said he would call the police and I said "but you ain't coming in until I see some ID". So, he did phone the police and about a quarter of an hour later with him still out in the rain two police cars and five coppers turned up sirens going obviously because my name had been mentioned. The copper said to me "What is going on and what is the problem?" I said that he wants to come in and search the unit and I also added that he isn't coming in until he has shown me his ID I am the manager and will not let anyone in without identification. He turned to Graham and said, "why don't you show him your ID " to which he answered, "because he knows who I am!" The police said to him that they could not waste anymore time coming down here will you please show him your ID so that you can go and look around the factory unit. This he did and I said thank you, you may go in now and look around. With that the police went to follow him in and I said "excuse me, before you lot go in I would like to see your ID cards as well" They were not too pleased as they knew I was taking the p out of them, about ten minutes later he got told off for wasting police time and they all disappeared. Graham the Fisheries Officer went away very embarrassed with his tail between his legs as he couldn't find any oysters, they were well on the way to the mainland.

On 1st November I was down at the marina every evening weighing the oysters in with the same fishery officer stood next to me checking the catches. It was highly amusing, as he did not say one word to me or Paul or Mike. We didn't say a word either. Every time he would put his hands in to check for undersized oysters I would tip another bag of oysters on top of his hands. It did cut them quite badly at times. We were still out clam fishing and also tons of winkles plus a colossal amount of oysters were going through our unit.

That year the manager's husband of the caravan park died. We had by this time bought Mobile home 5 that was making our business quite big. It was also time for me to take action to get rid of his wife and son. That year we had to work in the week we were off as we had great big tides, which meant we could hit on the clams, so we decide to have a few extra days off at the beginning of January.

2007

At the start of the year it was pretty much the same as previous years, the only difference being that this year was a lot milder so it meant that we could continue working on the seafood and clams

By 1st March we were down at the site to sort out our 5 mobile homes before holidaymakers arrived. Sue Ward, the manager had disappeared up north somewhere, the managing agents could not get hold of her, and no-one could go into the bungalow as it was full of her belongings. The only person who could and did go in was her son Stephen. This went on until the September when Peter Bohm called me out of the blue and asked if I could stand in as manager for the site. We had to stay in one of their Mobile homes as all of ours we were fully booked and of course we couldn't use the bungalow. This carried on until the end of October when we moved back to Binstead.

During that autumn the poaching continued and of course all the seafood was still coming in. At Christmas I was talking to my Uncle Norman and Aunt Ethne in Canada. They wanted to invest some money and asked how the business was going. They seemed very interested and within a month had purchased 2 mobile homes that were for sale on the site. Of course Terry Blake and myself set about making them look good with new decking etc as Uncle Norman had said he was going to come over in April to have a look. Straightaway we were taking bookings for him and he couldn't believe how much money was already going into his bank account over the winter months. Suddenly the mobile homes on our site were selling for very good prices so a few people decided to sell. My cousin Peter from South Africa wanted to buy one and another cousin David from Oxford had moved to the island and wanted to go into partnership with me. Well, I managed to buy one for Peter, two for David and me unfortunately at the higher price but at least we got them. It was certainly looking like 2008 was going to be a very busy year and we couldn't wait to get on with it.

2008

As soon as we got into the New Year it was all systems go as regards the Caravan Park. it was total chaos everything seemed to be looking good. We had 4 days off over the New Year, which now that Sue Ward was no longer in charge the atmosphere changed. All the owners wanted to get into their caravans to get them up and running but in previous years they had not be able to. They were not even allowed onto the site. All the electricity was turned off but I made sure it was switched on for them.

The two that David and I had bought together were also getting booked up. We decided to call the business Beachside Holidays Ltd. Cousin Peter came over from South Africa for a month and we helped him put decking all around his mobile home and to fit a new shower. Again it was quiet for the first couple of weeks so we made the most of it; we were having some great times there with the other owners. The atmosphere seemed so lovely and peaceful now that the Wards had gone.

In the June Sue Ward went bankrupt and decided to stay where she was in the north of the country. Everyone was so happy to hear this news, they were so sick of hearing Derek Ward bellowing across the site, how he never got a smack in the mouth I cannot imagine, probably because he was poorly or just grossly over weight, but all the owner were quite pleased that he had died.

We met some amazing people that summer and even now we still keep in touch.

The unit where we had our holding tanks was closing down at the end of the year, which was fine with me as I had other plans afoot. In the May of this year I bought a takeaway business in Sandown seafront called Sandown Bay takeaway Ltd. At the time it was just selling shellfish and looked quite scruffy. Not for long I should add, Terry Blake and I completely rebuilt it inside and painted it all so that it looked lovely. I also put a brand new double chipper and a griddle and microwave and in fact everything that went into making it a fabulous business. We opened in June and straightaway we were taking lots of money.

The business would stay open until 6 th November and then we could close for the winter until a week before Good Friday. During that summer the van was open from 9am to 11 pm.

On 1st August I decided to buy a kebab shop in East Cowes, it is the smallest takeaway on the island but had the biggest menu and was very busy

The clams, oysters and winkles were still coming in but we had stopped dealing in Lobsters and crabs as we only had a garage to store the stuff in.

In the first week of November we were able to get into the bungalow. What a disgusting state that was in. There was grease and knocks all over the worktops so straightaway I ripped the whole kitchen out and and rebuilt it all to make it liveable. I put a new cooker and hob in as well. Had to pay her £500 for all her belongings but I knew I would be dumping everything. We soon got it liveable.

We also had a list of people that wanted to buy a mobile home as they had found out how good it was there. The prices were really going up there. All the owners wanted to buy new caravans and get rid of their old ones so at the start of November until the following March we had to swap over 20 mobile homes, do all the pipework, electrics and gas work and also in the same four months Mike Terry and Ian Blake from Gosport built 22 deckings which also included lots of concrete to be mixed and put down as bases.

Later that month Mike, Rachel, Graham Wheeler and myself went over to Southampton to watch and follow the QE2 Cruise ship all the way down Southampton Water and out into the Solent as she was going to Dubai for her permanent mooring after 44 years in service in this country. Over her life she had done over 3 million miles. She was now to be used as a floating hotel. In my opinion she was always and still is the most beautiful ship in existence. The red funnel ferry was charted for this three hour trip and to see all the fireworks as the QE2 set sail. Quite an emotional night as we had all sailed on her; I had been on her 9times

Terry and Ian were coming over from Gosport every day at first light to help Mike and I. We worked right up to Christmas Eve to try and get as much done as possible. The weather did not help at all. It was windy and cold and we had so much rain, which of course made the ground so soft, and trying to move the mobile homes around became an absolute nightmare. We had Christmas day and Boxing Day off and then straight back onto it as we knew everything had to be done by 1st March and we never knew what the weather was going to be like in January and February. Sheila was working at the galley 4pm till midnight every day, clams winkles and oysters were coming in, and although was well needed then we were all set for 2009

2009

After taking a few days off at the beginning of the year we got straight back to work moving mobile homes around, building decking etc. We hired a JCB to level out the ground at the end of it we also changed the car park making it level and put a nice rope border around it, which gave us more parking spaces. We also put central heating in the bungalow where we were living.

The shellfish was still coming in fast so this necessitated my making a couple of journeys each week to the mainland to deliver it.

In January and February the weather wasn't too bad so we were able to get on and never lost any time due to bad weather.

The galley takeaway was doing exceptionally well probably because of the fact that it was the only takeaway open in East Cowes at the time.

We were taking so many bookings for the caravans but I must add that the site itself in January looked more like Beirut but we carried on and managed to get all the work done with 10 days to spare before the start of the season on March 1st.

Terry and Jill came over from Gosport to give us a hand. They stayed in one of our mobile homes for a couple of weeks. As Easter was closing in on us it was time to sort out Sandown Takeaway Ltd although it was thoroughly cleaned in November it still needed to be spuced up and given another total clean. We opened a week before Good Friday and it got so busy as we had introduced more stuff to the menu.

Sheila and I did manage to get away for a few days on the Arcadia with a couple that owned a mobile home on our site. We needed the break and when we returned it was all go again. By now of course the bungalow had been completely renovated with new kitchen, bathroom and full central heating so it was very comfortable for us. The summer flew by and once the children had gone back to school after the summer holidays we were back to autumn. The site close down 31st October for the winter to reopen on 1st March which meant there wasn't a great deal of work to be done during the winter months. The only thing we did have done was a 40 foot sewer tank fitted on the site. Adam Frampton and his building company fitted this.

That year there was tons of shellfish coming in so this meant that we were delivering to Portsmouth Seafoods in Havant three or four times a week. In September and October we were out poaching in the Solent and when the season started in

November there was an incredible amount in the Solent again.

Christmas came on us again with all the usual celebration

2010

At the beginning of 2010 the weather was horrendous. There was nothing we could do about it but carry on, onwards and upwards.

By the time we reached the end of February all the mobile homes were ready for opening on 1st March. We were already fully booked for the coming season.

In the April it was my 50th birthday but as the tides were big that year I had to work then. This involved being up at about 5.30 am for 2 to 3 hours and again at 6pm for the same amount of time. At the same time there was other jobs that needed to be done like getting stock for the Galley and Sandown takeaway. I was also getting some work for the gardener, David Lockyer to be getting on with. Really it was just like my other birthdays, my 18th, 21st,30th,40th then my 50th all spent working.

In May we started a dig in Newport, which proved to be very rewarding and we were able to add plenty of bits to our collections. It involved hiring a JCB again and of course we had to pay the farmer for renting his land. Fortunately, David Orman spent quite a lot of time with us on that dig and also purchased anything that we didn't want which helped pay the expenses. Although the dig was only for a few weeks it proved to be very profitable

That summer went very well, the weather was good, Sandown was taking a lot of cash and was really proving worthwhile. Sheila was running the Galley 7 days a week through the summer but was suffering very badly with arthritis in her hands and so we decided to take on more staff to help out.

We went on another cruise on the Arcadia that was good for both of us.

During September and October we were digging old bottles at Wroxall and again this proved profitable. Things were very good for us, we were meeting lots of new people on the site then disaster, Prime Estates the managing company for Rotch Property Group that owned the site started to get people interested in buying it as it had been on the market for 22 years whilst the other managers the Wards, were there but now the site was making a profit people were coming from all over the country to view the site plus Warners site next door. We had some lovely people come down to view and all seemed very interested. After this some others turned up from a company called DarWins who were the managing company for Kleinwort Benson Ltd. In the November they made several trips down to view and I was hoping they would not buy as they really didn't have a clue what it was all about and what the island needed, all they wanted to do was take all the trees out put roadways in and big fancy fences in and all the rest of the rubbish that goes with these so called experts that are good at spending other peoples money, some of the ideas they were coming up with were ludicrous, bloody stupid and ridiculous. I knew at that point that if they were going to take over I would be leaving the site and selling my mobile homes. All of the other owners were shocked at some of the ideas that were being put about and decided that they would sell their mobile homes and the prices started dropping drastically. Unfortunately, we knew that they had put in a bid but would not know if it had been sold until January 2011.

Tons of shellfish was coming in, poaching was brilliant in September and October and the main oyster season was good but we didn't enjoy Christmas as we had a lot on our minds. We knew that we had to make the best of it and wait until 2011 to see what happened

2011

Our thoughts were running high in anticipation as to what was going to happen at the caravan park. We knew that we would hear some news anytime soon. When it came it was not good news at all. DarWins had bought both the caravan park plus the old Warners site next door. All of us were totally gutted and knew that we would be off soon. We held a meeting at the Sherborn Centre in Binstead where I announced that I would be leaving the site. I sold my mobile homes for a lot less than I bought them. Luckily Uncle Norman from Canada and cousin Peter from Africa had sold theirs a few months previously so at least they were okay as was Bill and Julie Chittil

DarWins did offer me the job as site manager but I declined this offer as they wanted me to wear a suit which was absolutely ridiculous as the site was in the woods. Then for some crazy unknown reason instead of giving us two months notice to move out of the bungalow they got the dates wrong and put 2012 instead of 2011 so we stayed put for another eight months and they had to pay all our bills, how stupid some companies are.

Following this, out of the blue came a call from Prime Estates stating that the old house at Woodside Bay was up for rent. This house had been built in 1630 and was situated at the site of the 1969 Pop Festival where Bob Dylan and The Who performed. We moved in and did stay for a few years. The moon landing also happened in 1969.

Meanwhile we started clearing the land that I had bought in 2010 at Woodside Bay which was half an acre, and now that I no longer had to worry about the caravan park I was able to get on with it. There were 11 scrap cars and tons of bricks and rubble and rubbish. The barn had fallen in and was full of complete rubbish so we ended up having a fire going outside for six or seven weeks. There were some pigsties made of concrete that been built in the 50's which we cleaned out. Terry came over from Gosport and put a featheredge fence right around the land and secured the gate. After which we bought six pigs that could wander free on the land to dig and eat all the roots and anything else that was in their way. As the winter approached we rebuilt the barn as well.

The galley takeaway was doing well that year as was the Sandown Bay takeaway. Shellfish was coming in as well. It was an odd sort of year unfortunately things were not going too well for Sheila and I that year. We had our Christmas break which took us into 2012

2012

Right at the start of the year Sheila and I split up after 27 years together. My own thoughts on it were that we just grew apart but unfortunately Sheila believed that I was seeing another woman.

One night she came upstairs whilst I was on the computer, that night I was looking through some photos that a friend had put on Facebook. Her name was Paula and we had been friends and that was all for quite some time. She had 9 children and they all used to come down to Sandown to the takeaway. In fact on one occasion one of her children had lost their mobile in the sand and I had rung Paula to let her know and had then rung the phone and actually found it in the sand. There was nothing going on between us at all.

However, Sheila stood at the back of me accusing me of having an affair with this woman and then stormed out of the house. This was a totally different woman to whom she thought I was having a relationship with anyway but there was no talking to her at that point. She left the house and went and stayed with Mike and Michelle for a few months before finding her flat in East Cowes. She did change the story somewhat, which resulted in Mike and Michelle and my parents not talking to me. They would never believe that Sheila had got it wrong. It didn't bother me at all as I felt the relationship was over but more importantly I sold the Galley takeaway, as I didn't have anyone that could be in charge of the place.

I spent the next few months on the beach, which was busy with lots of clams, oysters and winkles, which were flooding in. I had a great team of people working with me.

In the April Mike turned up at the old house out of the blue. It had taken three months before we all started talking again. Whether it was because Mike realised that what his mum had said about me was wrong or not I don't know and I guess I never will know. Sheila did on a few occasions give an impression that she wanted to come back to me although nothing came of it. I don't think she liked to admit she had made a mistake.

It was all systems go for Sandown Bay takeaway in the spring of that year, it became very busy right from the start so, I decided to pack in the shellfish until September which gave the stocks of shellfish time to recover. We had a wonderful season down on Sandown seafront and we carried on until 6th November. We did start back on the shellfish in the middle of September that carried on until Christmas.

During this time I also concentrated on the farm, concreting the barn floor and made everything good. The new mobile home was all up and running and connected to all the services. I got 200 chickens and bought them a huge chicken run and two large sheds for them to rest in overnight. The pigs were doing well and also eight pigmy goats. The farm was looking good by this time. In the December Sheila, Mike, Terry and Joe from Gosport and myself cleaned and scrubbed the old house and I moved in to the mobile home on the farm. By now I was seeing Ellie Butchers who was the person Sheila thought I was having an affair with earlier in the year. Ellie and I have known each other since the 70's and used to chat on Facebook occasionally.

That Christmas I spent time alone with my animals, which was lovely. I made sure I had lots of food etc and relaxed over Christmas and New Year before starting off again in 2013

January this year was very cold but with some snow so all in all it wasn't too bad and we were able to work the beaches without any drastic problems. Unfortunately I couldn't do a lot on the farm as the ground was still very wet but I had the Takeaway to look forward to in April. We were busy all through the summer months and it was certainly making a good profit and kept my staff and myself very busy. Mike and Michelle were also very busy with their company Isle of Wight Bouncy Castles Ltd. Young Ellie was also helping during her school holiday and she loved it.

The usual chaos ensued over the August Bank holiday. There were lots of people around including all the scooterists that come over every year. Some of their bikes were fabulous looking machines.

They always spent well with us over that weekend; we were open until gone 3am in the morning and then back again at 8am the following day. On the Sunday I managed to get to see the start of the Cowes/Torquay/Cowes Powerboat Race, which is always an amazing site to see. After the children went back to school it was time to start back on the beaches. I had left one member of staff at Sandown to work from 9am to 6pm whist we were all on the beach. We closed the Takeaway on November 6th as usual after the amazing firework display on Sandown Pier. Again I spent Christmas, alone which was lovely, I would watch TV and listen to music with the animals up until the New Year when it was time to get ready for 2014

2014

This year was a pleasure to be able to get on with work at the farm. Also we had a couple of the goats were pregnant. I delivered those baby goats, which was an amazing feeling.

The shellfish was coming in but we had almost finished the clamming down at Newtown, as it needed a few years to reproduce. We then found a huge amount of Palourdes in the river Medina that were fetching good prices. Mike, Terry, Ian Blake, Mick Cox, Craig Nugent and myself were in the river for two tides for about 11/2 hours at a time earning great money.

Sandown Takeaway opened as usual just before Easter.

I was at the takeaway one day when a woman came by with two dogs one of which looked like a border collie. As I have always liked that breed I spoke to her and invited her to have a cup of coffee with me. We sat there, her name was Mimi and she explained that she was at present going through a break up with her partner and couldn't afford to keep both dogs. She also explained that the little one I thought was a border collie was in fact a cross between a cocker spaniel and border collie. She was a lovely dog and straightaway I said I would have her. However, the lady in question wanted to think about it so she went away armed with my phone number. With a couple of hours she had phoned and I asked if she wanted any money for her which she said no she didn't and the next thing she brought her down and from then on she became my little Lexi. She has been there for me since then, a reason to go out and down to the beach, a reason to carry on in actual fact.

At the farm more of the goats were becoming pregnant I ended up with 14 of them. One night when I came home I could hear a door banging and I knew it would keep me up all night if it continued. It must have been about midnight when I went to shut it. I went into the goats run and immediately trod on something that turned out to be a nail. This nail went through my shoe into my heel and into my heel bone. It did hurt quite a lot but being me, I didn't take much notice of it. I went indoors had a shower and sat down with a nice cup of tea and started phoning round and putting in orders for stock for the takeaway for the following day. By this time it was 1 am and I knew I needed to get some sleep in as I intended getting up at 5.30am. The following day I felt quite ill and decided to ring Sheila and ask her if she could stand in for me for the day. She was working part time anyway, so after a while I drove down the road to meet her and give her the float and any stock from the freezers at home. It was only a mile to drive but I was feeling lousy, I got back home and collapsed on the bed and went to sleep. I had a couple of days off but then decided to go down to Sandown just to sit and relax, as my foot was really hurting. I took the bandage off and my heel had started to be eaten away and there was a huge gaping hole there. The smell form it was disgusting as it was rotting flesh. Sheila advised me to go to the hospital straightaway. I drove back home and one of my staff drove me to the hospital. The podiatrist couldn't believe the state of my foot and three of them became very concerned as I am a diabetic and had lost all feeling in both of my feet and lower legs so of course I was unable to feel the true pain. I had to go back every other day so that they could try and make it better and certainly stop it getting any worse. The doctor told me that I was most certainly going to lose my leg I can remember saying to him I had been planning on losing some weight but not like this!

Every other day I went up there whilst they dug out the rotting flesh with a scalpel. The smell was awful, I can remember it well and the doctor said he was going to have to amputate it below the knee on my left leg. I still have the letter that would have been sent to my doctor saying the same. This carried on until the September when one day I walked into the hospital thinking that this was the day I was going to have to stay in and have it off. When they took the bandage off it didn't smell as bad as it had done. They started taking away the old flesh and I suddenly yelped, they had hit a fresh piece of flesh, they took a good look at it they decided that it must have started growing back again. They made it as clean as they could and sent me back home. I couldn't believe it, my leg was suddenly on the mend of course I had to return to the hospital at least three times a week so that they could check it and have the dressing changed. This went on up to Christmas before I was given the all clear, which was a close shave that really was. I was unable to work of course but Sandown Takeaway had been good all summer and there was plenty of shellfish coming in I was still making a profit. We had a great Christmas that year and were really looking forward to 2015

2015

My foot was a lot better by this time and I was able to help out on the beach with the other pickers up until April when I opened the Takeaway. In the March I had met Chrissy Pengelly, we spent a lot of time together and every weekend as she worked in Southampton. I used to pop over to Southampton every Wednesday and she would come over to the island on a Friday till Sunday. We were very happy together.

That summer was good the weather was beautiful then all of a sudden my sight started to go. I needed to get home quickly and managed to make a few phone calls. Thank God I didn't kill anyone en route. When I arrived home it went completely. It was a very strange feeling to go from good sight to absolutely nothing in just a few hours. A couple of days later my sight came back but not enough to read or drive. Luckily Chrissy was here for most of the summer holidays so she would drive me wherever I needed to go. At the end of the summer she needed to get back to Southampton but really didn't want to be there and decided to leave her job and move over in October at the end of term. We had some wonderful times together as we both shared the same interests. I met her family and also went down to Cardiff for her dad's 80th birthday we had a great celebration with all of her family. I had also booked a cruise for us and her daughter and boyfriend in the November. Chrissy's first grandchild was born and although we were going over every week to see the family she was finding it quite difficult being away from her children and grandchild. Things were good between us, we had a lovely cruise and apart from my sight the time was building up towards Christmas. Just the two of us were here it was lovely and then her daughter and boyfriend came over and spent a few days with us.

Sandown Takeaway had made a lot of money that summer but not knowing what was going to happen with my sight in the future I had to make some decisions whether to sell up or stay working there with all the dangers that could produce.

2016
By this time my eyes were not good at all and even though I had purchased a new catering trailer and

was having it all done up professionally with all the characters from Only Fools and Horses only it was being called Only Foods and Sauces. I decided to hand it all over to Mike and Michelle, as I knew I was unable to sort it out and get ready for the summer season. I certainly couldn't run a business where I couldn't work in it. At this time the absolute crooked, thieving disgraceful Isle of Wight Council also decided to increase the yearly rent from £832 to £5000 a year. For an area like Sandown where nothing was being done it was disgraceful. It is a known fact that the Isle of Wight Council are the most corrupt in the country as far as I am concerned. It has been talked about on the TV; several remarks have been made about this.

However, I was then set another huge blow as Chrissy wanted to return to her little house in Southampton so that she could be close to her children and granddaughter. I know it was a hard decision she had to make.

There was nothing I could do about the situation she left on January 17th and I have never spoken to her to this day.

Mike and Michelle were very busy with the bouncy castles and now running the Sandown Takeaway as well but at least they kept one of the staff on who had been a loyal employee for a few years. Quite often I would go and sit over there with them for the day and Mike and Michelle would bring me home at the end of the day.

I then met someone else who was very pretty and seemed to be an honest and truthful lady, we got on so well for months. She lived in West Sussex, I saw her every weekend and when she surprised me by saying she wanted to marry me, I was quite taken aback as I had never been married before. I said ok let's do it, she moved over to be with me but also bought her teenage son with her. He was the most ignorant, horrible gobby little devil you could ever imagine. I kept quiet about the situation and treated him like a bottle of good wine in the hope that he would mature with age. We decided to get married in the November and leading up to the day things didn't seem to be right and after a few chats with my son and a few friends I knew that this wedding was going to be a disaster. As I had already paid for it if nothing else I thought we could have a good party with plenty of food and drink. Everybody came, all my friends and family, we got married, the reception and a disco. It was so nice to see all my family and old friends who were getting quite elderly there. I have in fact lost some of them since.

The day after the wedding her son went off to the mainland with her daughter, whilst her dad stayed with us for a few days.

After those few days were up we took him back home to the mainland. On the way back things were really nice and even on the ferry we were planning what we were going to have for dinner etc. We went back to the farm and as we got home and went up onto the balcony, Mandy threw her arms into the air and said "Yes" I said "What" to which she replied with "I have never owned anything in my life but now as we are married I own half of this farm, your businesses and everything else you own half of it is mine and there is nothing you can do about it." Well, I was totally shocked, couldn't believe what I was hearing but I had something to tell her "I am so sorry to disappoint you, but I don't own anything, as the businesses belong to Mike, the farm was bought for Mike many years ago and he is the rightful owner" Well all I can say is I have never seen anyone have a total meltdown like she did so with that she got her dog and left. We had only been back about 20 minutes. Apparently, she walked round to the ferry terminal, got on a ferry and I never saw her again for a couple of weeks.

I had a kidney stone which was giving me so much pain that an ambulance had to come and take me to hospital, I was on Morphine at the time to help with the pain. She contacted me asked why I was in the hospital and said that she would be over on Tuesday 14th December with a man and van to collect all of her belongings. I said this was okay as I was going home on the Monday so would be there. On the Friday when Mike came to see me he was told he could take me home. So off we went and when I got home I found that my so called friend Jackie had been in and packed all her stuff because they thought I wouldn't be home until the Monday and they would sneak over on Saturday and pick it up. Jackie I believe had also stolen my pot of £1 and £2 coins that must have had £250 in it. I had to go straight to bed as I was heavily drugged up on Morphine.

I slept through the night and in the morning I heard some voices outside which turned out to be hers and someone I considered a friend of mine-not anymore I should add. They had broken the gates to the property and were trying to get into my home not realising I was inside. I put on some clothes and suddenly opened the door. They were shocked to see me there so I marched them both to the gates and threw them out telling her that the agreement was for her to come on Tuesday and Tuesday it had to be. She then announced that she would phone the police if I wouldn't give her her belongings. I told her to do it, which she did and sure enough after about ten minutes I could hear all the sirens, three police cars and a van because my name had cropped up. The coppers came in and asked if she could have her stuff and I then showed them the text saying she would be over on the Tuesday not on the Saturday.

I then also explained to them that I had just come out of hospital and really was unwell. I said she could take all her damaged and broken furniture from the barn but she was not going to take anything from my home. She was absolutely gutted, as she knew she had put her foot in it big time. Of course it had cost someone a lot of money to come over from the mainland. I found it quite amusing and it also proved that Jackie was no friend of mine. On the Tuesday she never turned up for all her things and her sons belongings so I messaged her and gave her another two weeks to collect them otherwise I would dispose of all of it. Well, she never turned up, I know she had read the message, she then sent me a message saying shove it so every single item of clothing, family photos, passports, medical cards, electrical equipment furniture, cutlery, everything you would own in a house I burnt it or dumped it. I had so much pleasure in doing that that it didn't really bother me too much about the money that Jackie took off me and the wad of notes Mandy my wife had taken.

It was now the Christmas break whilst all this was going on. On 29th December I went away on the

Queen Elizabeth cruise ship for 5 nights with a lovely lady called Donna Marie. We came back on 3rd January, my friend Keith had looked after the farm whilst I was away in case she decided to try and get back in.

2017

After the crappy year I had in 16 there was not a lot I could do, my eyesight was bad and I started to think about writing a book about all the crazy things that had happened to me during my lifetime.

In the February I started dating Joy Alexander who was the daughter of the late Scrappy Jack. I knew him in the 70's as previously mentioned Jack dealt in Scrap Metal. We were getting on so well, she was so helpful as regards my eyes. We went on a few lovely cruises and with her help I was able to enjoy them to the full. We had some lovely times during that summer and as I have previously stated I had taken her to see my dad and he remembered her Father with the words "and he never cared where it came from either". The fact that my dad was suffering from Alzheimer's, at the time and couldn't remember very much at all as he was going through so much with the dementia that made it difficult for him. Joy was in tears and so was I; he actually could remember Scrappy Jack.

Later that year my two sisters and my mum decided to sell the Dad's bungalow and downsize to a smaller one which was totally against my fathers wishes. Both Mike and myself were disgusted as dad had built the bungalow and it was his home, his pride and joy. He knew every inch of it and anyone who has had to deal with Alzheimer's knows that the person who is suffering would feel disorientated going to a new home. It was a very cruel thing to do to him. To take him away from everything that he loved. My youngest sister was in charge, she was a paramedic so should have known better the older one being weak. Anyway the bungalow went on the market and there were quite a few people interested immediately. At about the end of September a couple decided to buy it and my sister talked my mum into buying a bungalow close to my elder sisters house on the understanding that she would help my mum look after dad. The move was set for 18th December; I suggested that they bring Dad down to me to stop the trauma of him seeing his furniture taken out of his home and to make the new place comfortable for him with everything familiar in place when he went there. They refused so I made sure I was there for the move. Not that that helped the bungalow was freezing cold, no furniture or even any running water or heating. There were so many trip hazards and lots of damp it was a disgrace. With that my Dad started crying he just wanted to go home. The only redeeming feature of all this was the fact that my eldest sister lived near and would be able to help.

What a joke that was! On the 22nd December it was my Dad's 86th birthday and on the 23rd December they organised for him to be put in a home called the Goldings in Freshwater at the other end of the island. I agreed to go with Mike my eldest sisters husband, as I wanted to know where he was going and make sure he was settled in. When we arrived we were met with some lovely people that worked in the home and I must say what a lovely place it is. There was a lot of paperwork to sort out and sign. I had to do this with the manageress on my own as my brother in law decided he needed to listen to the football results in the car. As you can imagine everyone was disgusted with the fact that his beloved home had been sold on the understanding that one of the daughters would help look after him and within a week had been sent over to the other side of the island where he knew no one.

I am sure I went to that home twice a day including Christmas and Boxing Day right up until 9th January. Over that Christmas it was costing me £80 in a taxi. Mike and Michelle, Sheila Joy and myself would be there but not once did the others go. One nice thing did happen when Dad was sat in the lounge one day a little Tabby came in glanced around the room and immediately went and sat on my dads knee. He loved it as he had always had cats. To cap it all, the manageress said that there had been a phone call requesting that I was not allowed to visit my Dad. I said that I would like to bet it had come from someone called Sarah on the mainland she agreed and we just laughed it off. Lynn, the manager said I was welcome there at anytime and we have you down as next of kin and first call! This made me feel really good as he was not only my father, he was also my best friend and partner in crime in fact he taught me everything I know!

We didn't celebrate Christmas that year as most of the time was spent with Dad. I also split up with Joy at this time but we became very good friends afterwards.

2018
Firstly my dad was taken to hospital following a fall he couldn't walk but kept trying and subsequently kept falling over. In fact he hadn't walked since the day they sold his bungalow. At the time my Dad had been paying both my sisters mortgages and of course once he was incapable of doing that due to his illness they needed the handout from the sale of the property.

Between us Sheila, Joy Mike and Michelle went to visit three beautiful nursing homes and we were all prepared to pay the top up required for Dad's keep but the other lot wouldn't hear of it and they decided that he was going to the most disgusting, filthy, horrible stinking dump called Fairhaven in Ryde. What it is like now I have no idea but at the time it really was disgusting, the staff were scruffy and seemed to spend most of their time outside smoking instead of looking after people who were there. They all had an attitude apart from one person Angie Cave who did her best under the circumstances. Again it was only my lot that visited every day but hardly ever saw any sign of the others apart from once a month or six weeks my mum would put in an appearance on a Monday night.

In the April I met a lady called Helen Smythers and straightaway we became a couple. Helen is a lovely girl she has just got a Havanese puppy called Winston Vernon. We spent some lovely holidays cruising including a three-week cruise around the Mediterranean. To this day we still remain friends.

Once my dad had been put into the home he basically gave up and started deteriorating rapidly. Helen and I were there to see him for a couple of hours about three or four times a week and the rest of the time Sheila, Mike and Michelle and Joy went. We could all see him going downhill and although it maybe wrong to say this I was wishing him gone, I knew he wouldn't have wanted to end up like that. We were called to the home on 3rd August because Dad had taken a turn for the worst and looked as if he might die quite soon. Sheila, Mike and Michelle and Joy had been up to say goodbye to him and Helen and I stayed there all through the day and then overnight with him. My mums sister and a few members of their selfish family put in an appearance for about half an hour two days before he died on the 5th August Sunday at 12.10pm – he had been suffering so much it was a relief to see him go. We then contacted Dennis Firth, a lifelong friend, who immediately came up to say goodbye.

Because of my mum and sisters shopping around to get the best deal on the funeral it didn't take place until 3rdSeptember. Some of his grandchildren were away on holiday, not that they cared about him considering they never came to see him when he was poorly, we didn't find out until a few days before the funeral. My mum and sister phoned me and accused me of stealing a photo of my dad that was hung on the wall at the nursing home. My mum then found it whist I was talking to my sister and didn't bother to apologise to me. I had to lick their boots to get them to play a song I chose called "Forever Autumn" that is very moving to everyone that was there compared to what they chose, amazing grace and over the rainbow. We were not even invited to the wake which everyone I spoke to afterwards said was disgusting, I have not heard or spoken to any of them since that day and nor have Sheila, Mike, Michelle or Joy and to be honest I feel that they killed my Dad after the way they treated him and what they put him through, the promises that they made that they broke it is just a disgrace especially that despicable sister of mine who lives on the mainland.

Life is a lot easier now if anyone asks about my mother or sister I just simply say No they got wiped out in a road crash, I will never ever speak to them again and I hope that they rot in hell. After the funeral we came back and had a barbecue at the farm and a bottle of champagne to toast my dad's departure, what an amazing chap and the most crooked man the Isle of Wight has ever known for all the gold and silver that he bought over the years. He always made sure he was one step ahead. I can remember when I was a kid the police would come, they would turn the house over and yet they could never find anything. A lot of the time they were stood on it. I can remember those days thinking how can these people be doing a job so badly. It was great and almost as if my dad was taking the P out of them.

That Christmas I spent a lot of time with Helen and had a lovely Christmas dinner with Mike and Michelle. Back in the July they had moved into a beautiful mobile home that they had bought in March and sited it on the farm, which is fabulous, as I am now virtually blind they are right next to me and it works so well.

I have had several injections through the main part of my eye quite a few times this year and at the beginning of July I had to have a large operation on my left eye. They have also had both my eyes lasered, which has left me still suffering with very little sight.

2019

This was the year that I decided to write a book! This way I could hope to have it published around the time of my 60th Birthday. I haven't been able to do a lot because of my eyesight, the first part of the year was spent with plenty of hospital appointments for more injections in my eyes and other surgery and then at the end of July I had to have another major operation on my left eye.

In June Mike and Michelle bought a lovely ice cream van and after putting up with all the regulations put by the council, they had to wait for 4 weeks before they could take it out on the streets, but straightaway they were making good profits.

Around this time we had some absolutely magical news that Mike and Michelle are expecting a baby on 17th January 2020. Fantastic news, I cannot wait to meet my second grandchild. Ellie my other grandchild will be 10 by then and I know she is equally looking forward to the new arrival.

I am writing this on the 18th September 2019 and we had some more fabulous news today and that was that my new grandchild is a little girl and is going to be called Lilly. Alexandra Mather who is writing this book was the first person outside the family to know about the new baby and all I can say Sandra is you got it wrong you said it was going to be a boy! I won!

Later that month my uncle Pete died up in Oxford. Unfortunately I could not attend as his wife was adamant that she only wanted very close family there. I don't know what other people thought about this fact but I was pretty disgusted as Mike, Michelle and I would very willingly have gone from the Island to Oxford for the day.

It is now November and I am so looking forward to seeing my new granddaughter at the beginning of January. We will all welcome Lilly Linda Sheila Towill into the world.

At the moment my eyes are a little bit easier than they have been but for how long I do not know. Over the past couple of months I have become very close to a beautiful lady called Susan Hone who has an amazing attitude to life and a fabulous personality.

This has helped me a great deal with the operations and injections and other work to my eyes.

My bottle collecting is still going well and from time to time I find another one to add to the collection.

It isn't very long now until Christmas and the New Year. On the 6th January I will be off on another four night cruise to Germany on The Queen Victoria, then away again on the 23rd February for a fourteen night cruise down to the Canary Islands. I have plenty to look forward to but not forgetting my 60th birthday in April. It is amazing how quickly the time passes these days. I love where I live on our little farm smallholding. It is so quiet and peaceful with a huge abundance of wild life.

I have thoroughly enjoyed every moment giving my friend details of my life. I appreciate all her help and support for writing this book on my behalf. Alexandra Mather has written two books already which I feel sure will be a success and well worth picking up a copy.

Thank you for reading my book and learning about life on the Isle of Wight – who better to tell everything that went on than a fisherman who knows all about the core values of the people who live there and their escapades.

Time to sign off now God bless you all

Trevor John Towill